Dyspraxia 5–14

Second edition

Dyspraxia is increasingly common in young children. This fully revised and updated edition of Christine Macintyre's invaluable companion explains the difficulties faced by children with dyspraxia in growing up and offers suggestions as to how these might be alleviated.

In this book the children themselves, along with their parents and teachers, talk about how the difficulties change as the transition is made from primary to secondary school.

Children with dyspraxia are frequently beset by frustrations as a result of their differences, can be misunderstood both at home and at school, and are very often bullied. This practical guide considers:

- the issue of giving children labels;
- strategies to reduce stress;
- the value of movement programmes;
- raising self-esteem;
- the transition to secondary school;
- particular challenges faced during puberty/adolescence;
- handwriting as an indicator of dyspraxia.

Including practical activities with additional material for secondary pupils, this book shows children how to articulate their differences using individualised explanations, and then go on to succeed having recognised where their talents lie.

Dyspraxia 5–14 is essential reading for teachers, parents, SENCOs, teaching assistants and trainee teachers who want to improve their understanding of dyspraxia and its implications for children in Key Stages 1–3.

Christine Macintyre is an educational consultant, formerly at the Moray House Institute, University of Edinburgh. She is a prolific author, having written several books for Routledge and David Fulton.

D1335778

Other titles published in association with nasen

Dyspraxia in the Early Years (2nd edition)
Christine Macintyre
978-0-415-47889-2 (hbk)
978-0-415-47684-3 (pbk)

Teaching Foundation Mathematics: A Guide for Teachers of Older Students with Learning Disabilities
Nadia Naggar-Smith
978-0-415-45164-2

Language for Learning: A Practical Guide for Supporting Pupils with Language and Communication Difficulties across the Curriculum
Sue Hayden
978-1-84312-468-9

The Rob Long Omnibus Edition of Better Behaviour
Rob Long
978-1-84312-470-2

The Special School's Handbook
Michael Farrell
978-0-415-41685-6 (hbk)
978-0-415-41686-3 (pbk)

Beating Bureaucracy in Special Educational Needs
Jean Gross
978-0-415-44114-8

Living with Dyslexia (2nd edition)
Barbara Riddick (Forthcoming)
978-0-415-47758-1

A Handbook for Inclusion Managers
Ann Sydney (Forthcoming)
978-0-415-49197-6 (hbk)
978-0-415-49198-3 (pbk)

Listening to Children Read
Margaret Hughes and Peter Guppy (Forthcoming)
978-0-415-49836-4

Attention Deficit Hyperactivity Disorder (3rd edition)
Geoff Kewley (Forthcoming)
978-0-415-49202-7

Confronting the Obstacles to Inclusion
Edited by Richard Rose (Forthcoming)
978-0-415-49361-1 (hbk)
978-0-415-49363-5 (pbk)

Dyspraxia 5–14

Identifying and supporting young people with movement difficulties

Second edition

Christine Macintyre

LONDON AND NEW YORK

First published as *Dyspraxia 5–11* in 2001
by David Fulton Publishers

This edition published 2009
by Routledge
2 Park Square, Milton Park, Abingdon, Oxon OX14 4RN

Simultaneously published in the USA and Canada
by Routledge
270 Madison Avenue, New York, NY 10016

Routledge is an imprint of the Taylor & Francis Group, an informa business

© 2001, 2009 Christine Macintyre

Typeset in Baskerville by GreenGate Publishing Services, Tonbridge, Kent
Printed and bound in Great Britain by MPG Books Group, UK

British Library Cataloguing in Publication Data
A catalogue record for this book is available from the British Library

Library of Congress Cataloging in Publication Data
MacIntyre, Christine, 1938-
Dyspraxia 5-14 : a practical guide / Christine Macintyre. -- 2nd ed.
p. cm.
Includes bibliographical references.
1. Apraxia. 2. Movement disorders in children. I. Title.
RJ496.A63M327 2009
618.92'8552--dc22
2009004668

ISBN 10: 0-415-54397-5 (hbk)
ISBN 10: 0-415-54396-7 (pbk)

ISBN 13: 978-0-415-54397-2 (hbk)
ISBN 13: 978-0-415-54396-5 (pbk)

nasen is a professional membership association which supports all those who work with or care for children and young people with special and additional educational needs. Members include teachers, teaching assistants, support workers, other educationalists, students and parents.

nasen supports its members through policy documents, journals, its magazine *Special!*, publications, professional development courses, regional networks and newsletters. Its website contains more current information such as responses to government consultations. **nasen**'s published documents are held in very high regard both in the UK and internationally.

Contents

Figures

Tables

Foreword

It is indeed a privilege and a pleasure to be invited to write a foreword for the second edition of *Dyspraxia 5–14*. Christine Macintyre is well known as an author, and much sought after as a speaker and consultant in this area. She is well equipped to provide the type of updated information and insights required by parents and educators. Christine's books are always firmly grounded in research and provide the practical guidance essential for teachers and parents struggling to provide support for children with dyspraxia. Christine does not hedge on the issues and the practical advice offered in her books has been gleaned from a long and distinguished career in this field.

This second edition, I feel sure, will be as warmly welcomed as Christine's previous works. I am hearted to read that she has focused on the issues of learning differences as opposed to deficits. This is a crucial issue which impacts on perceptions of 'success and failure'; 'can and can't do' which often cloud the problem and undermine the potential of the many thousands of children with dyspraxia in the UK and elsewhere. It is important that teachers and parents recognise the attributes of individuals and their individual differences and seek to support children to maximise their potential. They may not end up as the 'David Beckhams of the world' but by recognising their learning differences and ensuring that they are supported through their challenges all children with dyspraxia can achieve. I am reminded of the number of famous authors, politicians and television personalities who are dyslexic and realise that it is not unreasonable that some young children with dyspraxia might overcome their difficulties and achieve in the same way, quite beyond current expectations.

What I pick up from reading Christine's second edition is the reassurance that 'yes' we do have programmes and 'yes' these approaches do work and 'yes' children with dyspraxia with sensitive handling, careful curriculum and lesson preparation will succeed. At the same time, Christine does not underplay these challenges. She talks about the need to develop self-esteem, to assist with developing self-organisation, to ensure that parents have strategies they can use at home to help the child with dyspraxia play a full part in everyday family life. It is also reassuring to read Christine's remark that 'it is never too late for intervention'. Yes, we all know that early intervention is crucial – for any learning difference – but it is reassuring to read that it is also never too late. This is a reassuring message to both teachers and parents who often, and sometimes unnecessarily, panic at the possibility of not providing the 'right' input at the 'right' time. If the input is right, the time is right. What can make a difference, as Christine rightly points out, is identifying the precise nature of the difficulties and the challenges. She acknowledges and, using very up-to-date information, discusses the often confusing overlap between dyspraxia and other syndromes. She also discusses the range of terms such as DCD and DAMP that can also cause confusion. Christine's informative and considerate take on this will be reassuring to many.

What makes Christine's books almost unique is that she utilises her background in research, stemming from her career in teacher education at Moray House, and her background in teaching and in physical education. In this book she provides informative perspectives on child development and gives an understanding of the stages and processes children go through when developing and consolidating learning. Her bio-physiological, cognitive and social insights into how children develop are encapsulated in Chapter 2, but in fact permeate through the whole book. These insights justify the practical advice offered in the book.

The other factor that makes this book a 'must have' for schools is the comprehensiveness in which Christine treats the subject. Every aspect is considered: the potentially vulnerable period of transition; parenting styles: develop policy; the learning environment; strategies for classroom management; psychological constructs and emotional and intellectual development. This strengthens my personal resolve that labels represent the 'beginning' and not the 'end' – they can provide pointers and guidance, but not solutions. One must keep an open mind when considering how to support children with dyspraxia, but importantly the decisions that are made need to be informed, based on knowledge, insights and recognition of the individual needs of children. Christine sets the record straight in this book and will provide confidence and inspiration to many teachers and parents looking for ways of tackling dyspraxia in the classroom and at home.

Dr. Gavin Reid
Consultant, Red Rose School for Children with Specific Learning Difficulties, UK
and Center for Child Evaluation and Teaching, Kuwait
Educational Psychologist, Vancouver, Canada

Acknowledgements

This is Hannah. She has dyspraxia. The book explains Hannah's movement and organising difficulties and shows how despite them, she remains a loving and lovely child. The book is written to help those who have children, who care for children, who teach children or who are children like Hannah, for she is not alone. The numbers of children with dyspraxia are increasing – or perhaps our awareness of the syndrome has caused us to identify more. Whatever the reason, it is imperative that all these children, and that means around 8–10 per cent of youngsters, are given specific help so that they may overcome their problems in the best way they can. Youngsters with dyspraxia may have a label – but that label need not endure, for although at this moment there is no cure, support in providing appropriate activities and regular, stress-free practice can make a huge difference.

Many children like Hannah have contributed to the compilation of this book. My thanks go to them and to their parents and teachers for allowing me to share in developing work that has been shown to help. With positive support and encouragement these children are realising that they are as capable and important as any other children. Understanding that dyspraxia is something they were born with and that having the difficulties dyspraxia brings is not their fault, they are gaining confidence and achieving more. When we have given them belief in themselves, and when we hear them say, 'Yes we can do it too', our job will be done.

Introduction

As children move from home, nursery or playgroup into the primary school, they face a significant number of new challenges and these increase in number and complexity as the years pass. As they approach secondary school the expectations placed on children's competence increase at a time when they are experiencing all the turmoil of adolescence. Increasingly, children must take responsibility for thinking ahead to organise their day, learning and practising new skills, completing pieces of work to a high standard and on time, looking out for each other and making friends. This is not an untroubled path for any child, but those with learning differences and specific difficulties need extra understanding and support if they are to reach their full potential and enjoy their time in school.

Children with dyspraxia come into this category. These children have a coordination disorder, which makes coping at home and at school both taxing and tiring. Without help they are sure to underachieve. Those who are there to offer the support they need must understand the complexities of dyspraxia, realise that it impinges upon all aspects of coping and learning, appreciate that progress will be erratic, no matter how hard the children try and, above all, help them to stay positive despite the frustrations that 'not being able to do' brings. This is the important message for everyone concerned. Stay positive. Recognise that all of these children can be helped. Children with dyspraxia are likely to be of average or above average intelligence. Their intellectual ability means that they can understand what is wrong, learn to keep their difficulties in perspective and understand how interventions are structured to help them; increasingly so as they mature. They also look just the same as other children. While this is a good thing, it also means that they can be denied the understanding that a more obvious disability would bring. 'If I had a broken leg, people would know and make allowances,' said Craig, adding, 'but some people still don't *know* what dyspraxia is!'

And so this book sets out to explain dyspraxia and how the condition impacts on children aged 5–14. Based on a developmental framework, it covers the myriad of influences affecting and affected by dyspraxia and emphasises how each child must be carefully observed and accurately assessed. This is to ensure that intervention can build on the young people's strengths as well as help them overcome their difficulties as far as they can.

The text also introduces the term 'learning differences' rather than saying learning difficulties or special educational needs, i.e. terms that implicitly suggest that these children have to be fixed; this term suggests that the environment at home and the curriculum at school have to be adjusted to meet the needs of the students who experience them. If not, then the differences will cause difficulties. It is interesting to note that in the Far East, where children learn to read using pictograms, there is almost no dyslexia. Perhaps a curriculum based on movement could ameliorate the lot of those who have dyspraxia?

So the text explains the competences that can be enhanced when movement is given a central place in children's learning. It also shows how a supportive environment with the correct resources, both human and physical, can both enlarge the repertoire of skills and relieve the pressures children experience. It offers many strategies to raise self-esteem because this is the foundation of learning. I hope that they do.

Chapter 1

Explaining dyspraxia

The Dyspraxia Foundation describes this learning difference as:

> an impairment or immaturity in the organisation of movement, which leads to associated problems with language, perception and thought.

This is a useful description but as it encompasses the whole condition, it is quite complex, and those who are interested in finding out about dyspraxia for the first time usually have a number of more basic questions. These require to be considered separately before the key issues are brought together again to show how apt the quotation is. If parents and teachers, and indeed everyone who is in close contact with the children, do not fully understand the condition and take the most appropriate steps to help, it is possible, even likely that all aspects of the children's development will suffer. This book has been written to provide that understanding and to show how the right kind of help can reduce the negative effects of having dyspraxia.

What do people want to know? The most usual questions are:

- What is dyspraxia?
- What difficulties do young people affected by dyspraxia have?
- How many young people are affected?
- What can be done to support the children at primary school and the young people at secondary, i.e. at adolescence?

Let's begin with the first question.

What is dyspraxia?

The name itself provides a brief description of the condition, for 'dys' means 'faulty' and 'praxis' means 'the ability to use the body as a skilled tool', and indeed it is usually a movement coordination difficulty of some kind which indicates that all is not well. Children with dyspraxia find moving easily (i.e. with efficient, flowing movements) difficult, especially when new challenges have to be faced. This may be caused by poor muscle tone that affects the children's participation in most activities of daily living. These children do learn to walk and run, write and talk but they often develop these skills – their motor milestones – later than others do, just within the 'normal' time span and they never quite reach the same level of performance. Practised movements do improve, and this is good news, which should give lots of encouragement, for it shows that intervention can be successful, but nonetheless they do have a fundamental insecurity with balance, coordination and control. This needs to be addressed early to maximise the chance of improvement.

There are many signs and symptoms that indicate that children could have dyspraxia and these will be discussed briefly in this introductory chapter and in more detail in the ones that concern each aspect of development. The aim is to give parents and teachers a comprehensive account of the condition. It must be stressed from the start, however, that it is not likely that any one child will have all of the symptoms! There is not one 'typical' dyspraxic child. Children have different blends of difficulties at different levels of severity. This can make accurate diagnosis quite tricky, especially as the children's 'performance', i.e. the level of success they have in tackling movement tasks, can vary depending on the setting, who is present and how the children are able to respond at that particular time. In addition, the things the children *can* do quite well can fluctuate from day to day. Teachers often say, 'but if he could do it yesterday – why not today?'; perhaps the child is too tired or perhaps, due to the short-term memory deficit which is a usual part of dyspraxia, he has forgotten the way he did it before. This is why it is important to make and record observations at different times of the day and in different situations. The fact that individual children have their own pattern of 'signs and symptoms' also means that one recipe for intervention will not do, for although motor programmes can be generally helpful, planning for specific, individual difficulties must also be carried through.

But if the difficulties are significantly interfering with their activities of daily living, the children may require more specific input than parents and teachers can provide. If this is suspected, then help from experts such as occupational, speech or physio- therapists should be sought as quickly as possible for waiting lists are long.

One 'positive' that is a comfort to parents and which should be remembered by every-one coming into contact with the children, is that they are likely to be of average or above average intelligence. Dyspraxia is not a general pervasive disorder. The Dyspraxia Association of Ireland (2005) quoted in Sweeney (2007) writes, 'Some children despite adequate teaching, a stimulating environment and a "normal" intellect have difficulty with movement and specific aspects of learning.'

So it is internationally recognised that children with dyspraxia do not have global developmental delay, i.e. an all-over low level of attainment. Their performance score is always well below their intellectual one. This means that affected children can understand what is wrong, how intervention works for them and how they need to persevere and practise, increasingly so as they mature. Children with dyspraxia also look just the same as other children and while this can sometimes deny them the sympathy that a more obvious disability would bring, no one would want them to have to overcome 'looking different' as well. Kirby (1999a) explains that these children have a 'hidden handicap'. This means that other people have to be able to recognise what is causing the difficulties and be prepared to learn how to help. Nor do they have a clear neurological disorder such as cerebral palsy or an illness that causes physical pain or gets worse. And so, although dyspraxia brings a number of problems and many frustrations, there are plus points, and appreciating these and remembering them when things get tough as well as building on the success that practice can bring, is the best way to keep morale and self-esteem high.

Sadly, at present there is no cure, although ongoing research, e.g. into the metabolism of fatty acids and in using coloured lenses or overlays to steady text and help spatial judgments as children with Mears-Irlen Syndrome do, is holding out hope that quicker and more successful ways to help are being found.

What difficulties do children have?

'Poor coordination' is a term that covers different kinds of actions. It depends on the interplay of different movement abilities such as perception, i.e. taking cues from the environment to guide spatial judgments, a good sense of both static and dynamic or moving balance and rhythmic awareness (more detail in Chapter 3). Moreover, there are different kinds of coordination depending on the intrinsic nature of the activity that is to be done.

First, there is whole body coordination that involves the large muscle groups and affects gross motor skills like running, jumping and climbing. Some children have great difficulty in doing these basic movement patterns. One cause is poor muscle tone. If this occurs in the pelvic region, running can be affected by lax hip and leg muscles.

Lax muscles allow toes to turn in and brush against the legs causing stumbling. To run *at all*, these children need to concentrate hard on controlling their feet to avoid falling, while other children race ahead without giving control a thought. Shoulder laxity prevents control of the arms and so any pulling action where strength is required is very difficult, for example, pulling along a bench while lying on the front takes much time and a great deal of body 'hitching along' to compensate. Children would also be likely to find the arm action in swimming ineffective.

It follows that when apparatus needs to be controlled, as in kicking or catching a ball or in batting skills, their difficulties are significantly increased, for these skills call on hand–eye or foot–eye coordination in addition to whole body coordination and this can be overwhelming! Controlling apparatus needs a clear sense of body boundary, i.e. where the body ends and the apparatus begins, as well as visual and spatial awareness to track the flight of the oncoming ball or to judge where to send it. Did you ever think that moving could be so complicated?

Then there is fine motor control that requires the smaller groups of muscles to work in harmony. If they don't, children will have difficulty writing, drawing, sewing and carrying out movements where precision is required. Having said that, children who find writing difficult because they can't find an effective pencil grip or because handwriting involves crossing the midline of the body, often manage keyboard skills with ease. In this activity there is no pencil to control and each hand works largely on its own side of the body. The

Observe how the poor muscle tone is affecting Liam's ability to run

children can sit upright and be well supported, their backs held by the chair; their feet should be planted firmly on the floor and the height of the computer should be adjusted to suit their size. Given these preparations, the children are freed to concentrate on the task in hand. This 'solution' to handwriting problems brings out another positive in that there is often a way to circumvent difficulties, and later in the book lots of suggestions are made in the hope that teachers will find them practical and realistic when they have numerous other children to teach as well.

Children with dyspraxia often hate having to be involved in sporting activities. It is hugely upsetting for children always to be the last to be chosen because they can't play well or can't follow the rules of the game. Having said that, some love to play. This can depend as much on the attitude of the other children as on the temperament of the child himself. Jamie explains, 'I'm not in the best team but a jolly good one. Sometimes I get a bit mixed up when we change ends but everyone just shouts, "Come on Jamie, this way!" Once or twice I've scored an own goal and everyone groaned, but when they saw I was upset the teacher reminded us all that it's only a game and what was the important thing to remember? That everyone should have fun.' So the school ethos can make a huge difference.

Not many children with dyspraxia can sustain his happy-go-lucky approach, however, and with the others in mind, the question must be, 'Do they have to play?' Could they not have an important 'other' job such as being the scorer or timing their own attempts at completing a circuit rather than competing with others? Or perhaps the children could have a choice of activities, so that they can choose something they enjoy – perhaps downloading information for the class theme from the Internet? Other kinds of activities can sometimes be substituted for those that are too difficult and so make a positive input to the children's day. The best thing is for small groups of children with the same interests to work together in a purposeful and enjoyable way. Then all the children can play a full part. Nowadays, classroom assistants could supervise these 'other activities' while the teacher is in the gym or out of doors. It would be wonderful if the stress that dyspraxic children feel acutely could be relieved in this way.

Middle childhood years – ages 7–14

In the junior and middle schools however, children usually have to join in a great range of activities, and this is why age 7–14 can be the most difficult time for children with dyspraxia. After that there is more choice and the children can choose activities to suit their strengths. This is helped by the fact that the developmental path is relatively smooth between ages seven and the onset of puberty. A set of important changes are happening but over time. However early puberty can add a whole set of new problems. This is difficult for most children coping with an onslaught of hormones and more so if there is a specific learning difficulty (see Chapter 8).

To ease stress caused by having to do tasks that are overwhelmingly difficult, it would be helpful to introduce choice much earlier. Perhaps teachers worry that if children with dyspraxia are allowed to miss activities like team games, the others will see them as being 'different' thus increasing their social isolation, or that the children will miss out on the very kind of activity they need. But, from the children's point of view, team games usually mean public humiliation, because they can neither follow the rules, carry out the required skills, nor understand the spatial dimensions of the game. Their potential level of participation is further lowered by the stress this brings. For these reasons this kind of activity is not helpful; these children need a small group perceptual-motor programme specifically designed to help their learning differences (see Chapter 9).

Verbal or oral dyspraxia or specific language difficulty

One specific kind of coordination requires the muscles in the lips, mouth and soft palate to work together to produce coherent speech. Children who can't articulate clearly have difficulty in making themselves understood and so they lose confidence in interacting and building relationships and as they hit the middle years they prefer to work and play alone. In the nursery the peer group can often understand indistinct speech when the practitioners can't and this eases interaction but as the children grow, communication is more verbal and children are perhaps less tolerant of those who cannot make themselves understood.

Sometimes children with dyspraxia have difficulty in regulating the tone or pitch of their speech and this can make them reluctant to communicate. This is verbal dyspraxia and for the children who attempt to talk before moving around, it can be the first indication that something is wrong. This is a very different problem to that faced by children who don't understand language and who therefore do not give the correct answers. Children with dyspraxia do understand, but they have difficulty controlling the 'technical equipment' so that it makes the correct response. This links back to the intellectual differences mentioned earlier. Slack muscles in the mouth can also cause dribbling that is socially frowned on. When children with this difficulty lean over their jotter to write, as one example, dribbling onto the page spoils their work and of course this is most upsetting for them. When they have to concentrate so hard on their writing skills, other areas of control tend to give. Having an inclined desk can reduce this problem because then the children don't have to lean so far over their work.

Two-handed coordination is often difficult for children with dyspraxia, especially if the movement task requires them to cross the midline of the body or take their hands behind their back. Tasks like opening a carton of juice or using knives and forks cause difficulty as do visits to the toilet – for this involves undoing buttons or zips, sitting comfortably balanced on the loo, then wiping before getting dressed again – a whole set of complex tasks, made much worse if they have to be done quickly at a certain time of day with another child waiting to go.

Crossing the midline presents huge obstacles for children with dyspraxia. All sorts of daily tasks are affected, e.g. pulling on socks, reaching over to open a door, buttering a roll on a plate, using a compass, retrieving a bus ticket from a wallet, even filling a basket in a supermarket! It is as if a wall divides the two halves of their body. Often these children also lack a sense of having a dominant hand and if they are asked to draw a rainbow they will use one hand for the first section of the arc then transfer the pencil to the other hand to complete the pattern. Getting dressed independently can be a nightmare. Unfortunately, children can regard this as a landmark of achievement in the primary school and those who can't are teased: 'He can't tie his laces yet.' This is another public declaration that is humiliating and hurtful. Many mums have had cause to bless Velcro for all sorts of fastenings and again this is an example of identifying the problem and then searching for ways to overcome it. Some schools however, won't allow Velcro fastenings for shoes and trousers and refuse to have elastic for school ties – and of course no child likes to be different. I wonder if these schools have understood dyspraxia at all? Would they listen if parents tried to explain?

Some children may only experience problems with movements that involve the large muscle groups. While their gross movements, e.g. running and jumping, are clumsy and awkward, they can manage fine movements quite well. Others only experience difficulty when fine motor skills are required; they do not have the dexterity to fasten buttons or do up zips. Not all children have articulation problems. Careful observation and recording of children coping or not coping in different situations is essential if intervention and help is to be targeted successfully. This continuous assessment and recording of encountered difficulties in different situations is essential before specialist help is requested. And of course the benefits and possible disadvantages of giving a child a 'label' and extra programmes of therapy have to be understood too (see Chapter 2).

Sometimes children have difficulties because of a co-occurring problem. Reid (2005) advises that diagnosis must take the presence of overlapping or linked conditions into account. He explains that the characteristics of other conditions such as literacy difficulties, attention difficulties and dysgraphia can overlap with dyspraxia. Kirby (1999a) also explains that it is very difficult to find the 'pure' child. She claims that 'almost half the children with dyspraxia will also have dyslexia; some will have an attention disorder (ADD or ADHD) or Tourette's syndrome'.

No matter what their difficulties are, all children can be helped to improve discrete skills, and this means that when the children are required to do these movements – given time and encouragement and sustained practice – they will be able to cope. Portwood (2004) points out that the manifestations of dyspraxia can vary with age and development, and so as children grow, remedial programmes tend to move away from general movement strengthening and exercises to promote dexterity to practise discrete skills such as cooking and other activities of daily living. But the movement analysis stays the same.

However, when children have to do even practised actions again in different environments, they have to tackle them as if it was their first attempt. This is because dyspraxia prevents transfer of learning from one situation to another; the children do not have the movement recall that allows them to select aspects of the movements they already can do and apply them in new situations. This means that movements do not become automatic; the planning for each one has to begin anew. When Ayres (1972) defined dyspraxia as 'the inability to plan and execute non-habitual movements', this is what she meant. As a result of this constant concentration – remember how difficult learning to drive was? – the children become tired and dispirited and when on occasions it all becomes too much, screamingly frustrated with all the effort 'just managing' entails. The frustration is made worse when they see other children coping with little effort and lots of success. And these others may not be so bright as they are. For youngsters with dyspraxia, the day is full of first-time challenges and so they have a very tiring day. For these reasons, those who understand dyspraxia will not urge these children to 'try harder' or to 'do it again, neatly this time', for they are likely to be trying just as hard as they can and repetition means more failure and more distress.

These coordination difficulties belong to the movement execution or 'doing' aspect of dyspraxia and they have been highlighted first because movements that are clumsy and awkward are the most obvious signs that something is amiss. There are two other facets, however, which may well hamper efficient movement. These are the planning and organisation of movement, i.e. the underlying intellectual processes which must be considered in any analysis of dysfunction or impaired action. Movement then, has three sub-components (Figure 1.1).

Figure 1.1 The three sub-components of movement

Knowing what to do

Children who have difficulty with this aspect of movement preparation can often be seen wandering around looking lost, or doing something aimlessly. Usually they stay on the periphery of any activity. This is because they are so unsure of what to do. Poor short-term memories also mean that they forget what they did before. They may try to copy other children, which can help up to a point, as long as their 'model' is successful in following instructions and as long as the copying causes no resentment. Copying does mean delay however, and if the dyspraxic child is already quite slow at responding to instructions, scolding may follow.

Planning

Planning depends on recalling previous events and using the feedback from these to amend or improve the new plan.

Children who are poor planners can know what they want to achieve, but have difficulty knowing how to bring their ideas to fruition. Planning involves building a mental model of the action: 'I'll have to jump over that puddle if my shoes are to stay dry so I'll run fast and then when I get near the water I'll swing my arms to help me jump', or 'If he hits the ball over there, I'll have to move out to the side to hit it back', or 'If I am going to construct this bridge, I have to find the span then decide on the number of supports … or in my story this idea will make a good ending'. This can be helped by adults asking, 'What is it you would like to do?' and then helping the children to remember and plan ahead. This is so much better than adults taking over and the children carrying out their plan. Youngsters have to retain ownership of their learning if it is to be meaningful to them rather than just rote learning. Unfortunately often the time pressure to get things done acts against this. Perhaps teachers and parents together could discuss times when this would be possible? In doing a project, for example, discussing the plan and what information should go where for one section at a time can ease the stress of trying to remember the whole.

Organising

Youngsters who are poor organisers have problems ordering the sequence of actions, in deciding what resources they will need, what action should come first, how long each part takes, how much strength and speed each action requires, or where they should go. Getting dressed, that is putting clothes on in the correct order, is really problematic for some children – this is different from not being able to do the intrinsic actions, e.g. fastening buttons. Sometimes children manage the first part of a sequence of actions or follow the first instruction, but then, due to poor short-term memory, they forget what comes next and either stop, bewildered, or 'do their own thing', which again is rarely appreciated!

If any of these difficulties are present, then it is not difficult to see that the children will need more time to sort themselves out. So often they are urged to 'hurry up', just to keep up with the others or to arrive somewhere in time. 'What is *valuable* time?' asked six-year-old Peter. Obviously he had been found guilty of wasting it. Having to hurry however, acts against movement being coordinated and so it is clumsy: the child misses the ball or collapses onto a chair, knocks it over and both clatter to the floor, or he misjudges the space between himself and objects and bumps into whatever or whoever is in his path. One fairly exasperated teacher wrote, 'You'll know this child, his shirt is always hanging out and when he rushes to say hello he is forever standing on your feet' – a picture that evokes a wry, if compassionate chuckle.

Executing

This concerns actually carrying out the movement with all the movement ability requirements such as strength, balance and control coming into play. Alongside that, the perceptual judgments that inform the action must be accurate (see Chapter 3).

Analysing planning, organising and carrying out movement

It goes without saying that when children have difficulties, movement analysis to find the exact reason must precede intervention. Correcting the movement pattern is only going to be of minimal use if, for example, the underlying strength is lacking. This is complex but essential if help is to be targeted correctly.

For those of us who do not have these difficulties, it could be salutary to take a moment to think of the planning and organising that children must cope with before they enter the classroom at all and before they have the support of any teacher.

This mini scenario opposite shows some of the more subtle implications of not being able to move well – it demonstrates the 'waves' that spread out to embarrass and confuse the child and negatively affect his self-esteem. Few seven-year-old children have the level of altruism or courage to stand up for a child who has dyspraxia, especially as that child, used to being mocked, may react inappropriately, not realising that a friend has come to help. The scenario also shows why 'the primary objective of all methods of intervention must be to improve the child's ability to function in everyday life' (Sugden and Henderson 1994).

This means that parents can play a huge part in helping, firstly through understanding the condition, then using routine tasks and everyday coping skills as practices. Realising this can demystify the 'treatment' and make it much more manageable for many parents. Specially designed therapies can be required for children with specific difficulties but many have no access to, or do not wish to have this kind of intervention. When children are tired, parents are anxious and siblings resent the time given to one child, therapy-at-home time can become fraught, with tears and storms and eventually it may be abandoned. Then everyone feels guilty and any hope of progress seems remote.

And of course, all children can be clumsy and forgetful and disorganised at times. The Dyspraxia Foundation urges us not to call every child who displays some of these characteristics some of the time, dyspraxic. Dyspraxia is an enduring condition and although some days are better than others, children, young people and adults have a consistently low level of motor performance. The American Psychiatric Association (1994) sets out five criteria for dyspraxia, the condition they call developmental coordination disorder (DCD). They are:

1   There is a marked impairment in the development of motor coordination.
2   The impairment significantly interferes with academic achievement or activities of daily living.
3   The coordination difficulties are not due to a general medical condition, e.g. cerebral palsy, hemiplegia or muscular dystrophy.
4   It is not a pervasive developmental disorder.
5   If a developmental delay is evident, the motor difficulties are in excess of those usually associated with it.

These can usefully guide any diagnosis of dyspraxia, in their terms 'developmental coordination disorder' or the condition in the Scandinavian countries called DAMP, i.e. disorder of attention, movement and perception.

Example

Picture Jack, aged nine, coming into school on a wet day. The normal routine of waiting outside has been disrupted by bad weather and the cloakroom is noisy with children bustling around divesting themselves of a multitude of anoraks and wellies. Jack must find his own peg, but today it has disappeared beneath a pile of coats. He doesn't want to ask for help or he might be teased and the noise is confusing him even further.

Then, he must get out of his wellies and put on his trainers. While he tries to do this, his boots get kicked out of the way. Really agitated now, he chases them in his socks, which get soaked and so won't slip into his trainers. The struggle to get them on means that he has to balance on one foot and cross his hands over the midline of his body. This is impossibly difficult and he has to give up.

Jack

After that, lunch boxes have to be placed in the correct place – where's that again? – and notes from ` have to be retrieved from his schoolbag and taken to the classroom. This means he must undo his schoolbag and because he clutches the bag tightly to his chest, all his books spill out onto the wet floor. Jack knows this will be discovered and he cries and so desperately wants to go home. The other children laugh and his books join the kicking game.

When Jack does get to the classroom, he discovers he hasn't left his coat in the cloakroom and he is sent back. By this time he is so unhappy that he is not sure whether the cloakroom is round that corner or the next one. He sits down for a rest and watches the infant children coming in, loses track of time and when the teacher sends someone to find him, he knows he will be scolded again – even though he's not sure why. Poor Jack! What a start to the day and it's not nine o'clock yet!

What additional features does DAMP cover?

Children with dyspraxia have difficulty in interpreting perceptual information, i.e. clues which come from the environment through the senses to be organised in the brain and then relayed to the muscles to produce efficient and effective movement (Figure 1.2). Their sensory input gives false clues so the beginning of the learning sequence is flawed. Those who use the term also highlight the difficulties youngsters have in paying attention. Other diagnosticians might see this as ADD or ADHD, a separate neurobiological condition rather than part of dyspraxia.

If the child's perceptual system, i.e. all the sensory information coming to the brain, is incorrect in some way, then the sequence of events that follow will be faulty too. If, for example, a child sees the table as being nearer than it really is, then the cup of juice which is to go on it crashes to the floor, whereas if he sees it as being further away, then he will be onto it before he can stop and bumping and clattering result. The child has not been careless; he has followed the spatial information he has received. This explains why everyday actions which happen in the same settings and therefore can be called routine, practised actions are much more efficient than new movements carried out in unfamiliar places. Habitual or practised movements provide feedback each time they occur and so the children gradually manage to make adjustments until the action is correct. This, of course, can't apply when movements are being tried for the first time and so these are clumsy, often causing irritation, even retaliation when bumping into others happens, or when spills down clothes or onto carpets occur!

A last difficulty that must be considered is that some children retain some of the primitive reflexes that should have been inhibited through maturation. Goddard Blythe at the INPP clinic in Cardiff begins any remedial works by assessing the presence of all the primitive reflexes because if these are retained, the postural reflexes that are required for more sophisticated movements cannot replace the primitive ones as they should. One example of this could be a child unable to sit still. If the hyper or over- sensitive areas on the bodies are stimulated, perhaps by a T-shirt rubbing, then movement, e.g. jerking the hip and shoulder together on one side, which is quite involuntary occurs – as much to the child's surprise as anyone else's. These movements, which are not under the conscious control of the child, may take the form of fidgeting, twitching or shoulder shrugging depending on the region that is activated. They can be very distracting to the teacher who has just settled her class and can as such be a source of negative input for the dyspraxic child. Another critically important one comes to light when children have handwriting difficulties, for it is likely that a retained ATNR (asymmetric tonic neck reflex) prevents crossing the midline. It is likely that these children will never have crawled using the cross-lateral pattern. Instead they may have bum shuffled or crawled using a homolateral pattern, i.e. hands and

Figure 1.2 Perception: an input/output model

knees on the same side working together. A key test for this is to ask children to crawl and observe their pattern carefully.

How many children are affected?

- 8–10 per cent of children have some degree of dyspraxia.
- 2 per cent of these children will be severely affected.
- Boys:girls are affected 4/5:1 but when girls have the condition, they tend to be more severely affected (Dyspraxia Foundation: 2007).

What does this mean? Well, for parents, these figures can offer some comfort in that they are not alone in having a child with movement difficulties. But they can be also be frightening or daunting if they show that another disorder could be making the diagnosis worse. Thinking positively however, this does mean that there can be more than one source of support and help. At this moment in time, more dyslexia than dyspraxia groups are established and so are further on in being able to offer support and advice. These could be a useful first line of enquiry. There is also more information in books now (see the Bibliography) and currently dyspraxia is getting more research support. The Dyspraxia Foundation is a major source of support.

Teachers will possibly find these figures startling because they mean that there are likely to be two, even three children with some degree of dyspraxia in every class. Many will deny this until they understand the condition and develop the eyes to let them see. In fact one teacher told me, 'Now that I know what to look for, they've all got it!' Many early years teachers have told me that they 'know there is something wrong', but they are not sure what is causing the difficulty and so they are reluctant to suggest to parents that their child has a problem. This is because the parents are likely to be upset by any suggestion that their child is not coping well and if the difficulty is caused by developmental delay, rather than dyspraxia, maturation, hand in hand with appropriate teaching, may well sort it out. The teachers, however, have to recognise the possibility that dyspraxia could be the diagnosis and take steps to intervene and help – after all fun activities for the whole nursery, e.g. songs like 'Head, shoulders, knees and toes' with the important addition, coming up the back, heels, bottoms, backs and nose, can be enjoyed by all the children, even though they have been specially chosen to help the youngsters who have poor body awareness and are not too sure where their knees and toes are. (Lots of suggestions to help this age group are in Chapter 9, and also in *Dyspraxia in the Early Years*, published by David Fulton Publishers, specifically written for this age group.) 'Simon says' can replace this for the older children and allowing the adolescents to teach/explain to/support the younger ones can mean they have repetition without feeling demeaned by the jingle.

But when the difficulties persist beyond nursery, time is no longer on their side. Children as young as six self-evaluate through comparing themselves with their peers and see themselves as incompetent. If they move clumsily or drop things, they arouse conflict and anger in adults. They know they have displeased but are not sure why, and so they think, 'What's wrong with me?' And once they begin to evaluate themselves in this negative way, they generalise this assessment to other aspects of coping and learning. They don't say, 'I'm a bit clumsy at writing', or 'I'm not good at football', but 'I'm no use at all'. They begin to believe they can't do anything well. And so teachers have a huge responsibility both in helping the children and in informing the parents who will decide if they wish to have their child tested by psychologists and, depending on the results, request physiotherapy or occupational therapy to help. There are also many classroom opportunities and strategies that can help these children – these are set out alongside the difficulties described in each chapter and in Chapter 7. By age six or seven, intervention is vital. Fun-to-do activities can be built into the classroom routine. Taking part will harm no other child. The sooner the intervention happens, the more effective it is likely to be. All children have a right to an education that allows them to fulfil their potential. Everyone must ensure that children with dyspraxia have this too.

The following chapters will go into much more detail and show the implications of dyspraxia for the children in each aspect of their development. They will give suggestions and strategies that have helped other children. At this moment in time, dyspraxia is claiming more attention from those who have the resources to help. We need to be sure that they are targeted in the right direction, i.e. to boost the children's self-esteem through making them more competent in their movement abilities. This will enhance their participation in all aspects of their development.

Children and young people with dyspraxia will have:

- difficulty in producing coordinated, fluent actions;
- a poor sense of balance leading to lack of control;
- difficulty in knowing what to do and judging what kind of response is acceptable;
- difficulty in retaining more than one piece of information, e.g. story sequences or any 'do this and then that' kind of instruction;
- weak muscle tone impacting on the execution of movement patterns;
- poor body awareness, i.e. knowing where the body parts are in relation to one another;
- poor kinaesthetic awareness, i.e. knowing where the body is in space, which affects spatial judgments e.g. how far and in what direction should I move?
- ipse lateral hand use, i.e. using the hand on its own side of the body;
- lack of clear bilateral dominance, i.e. no clear picture of a stronger side. Mixed dominance leads to directional confusion, i.e. reversal of letters, numbers and words and also difficulty in asymmetrical movements such as tying laces or using cutlery or holding paper in one hand while cutting out with the other.

The difficulties can appear never-ending and some unfortunate youngsters have lots. However, other children may only have difficulty in a few areas. All the children need lots of positive reinforcement when things go well and sympathy, understanding and tolerance on a bad day.

What can be done to help?

Once parents and teachers understand the range of difficulties their youngsters have, they will be anxious to remove all the obstacles they can from their home and school day. There are different ways to help, depending on the age of the children – newly-into-school children will need pictures and colour coding while older ones will be able to follow directional arrows or written instructions. These aids are time consuming to make at the outset, but this is time well spent as they do help the children to be independent. The children themselves can choose the pictures, decide on their favourite colour for colour coding and generally help prepare the resources, so learning about them at the same time.

The children's difficulties will be in:

* knowing what to do;
* getting organised; and
* getting it done.

And of course input must be helpful to the specific difficulties each child has. Parents and teachers need to anticipate what their children need to be able to do to 'get there' with as little stress as possible for everyone in the family.

What is the best way to do this? (See also Chapters 6 and 7.)

* Think of each part of the day separately and decentre, i.e. visualise the kind of hurdles children are likely to face.
* Identify the child's difficulties and prepare a checklist of 'things to be done' (see Table 1.1).
* Use colour coding whenever possible – red dots at home and at school help the children identify their own toothbrush, blazer, PE kit, Wellingtons, jotter, etc. and this saves both time and squabbles. A supportive teacher could have the child in the red group so that colour coding was not so obvious, or other groups might use different colours to help identify their work too.
* Use numbering to help the children follow the order of things to be done. The children could paint the numbers and Blu-Tack them, e.g. on their bedroom wall, so that clothes could be set out in the correct order, thus simplifying getting dressed.

Table 1.1 Organisational lists

Before school	Preparing for school	At school	Home and evening	Going to bed
Getting up				
1 Find slippers (easiest on a plain carpet) and dressing gown	1 Get dressed (follow code)	1 Cloakroom • put coat on peg • undo bag • take pencil and books to class • give money to teacher	1 Put shoes and coat ready for morning	1 Shirt and pants to the wash
	2 Pack schoolbag • pencil case • books • PE kit • money for bus			2 Clean teeth
2 Toilet			2 Change into play clothes	3 Get washed
3 Wash			3 Have a snack	4 Put pyjamas on
4 Go downstairs	3 Pack lunchbox • sandwich • drink • apple • crisps	2 Hand in homework	4 Play with dog outside	5 Go downstairs (slippers and dressing gown)
5 Let dog out		3 Collect silent reading book	5 Watch TV	
6 Have breakfast (cereal then toast)		4 Check tray for returned work	6 Homework	6 Say goodnight
7 Go upstairs and brush teeth			7 Supper	7 Go to bed

- Have a free-standing kitchen timer to help the children realise how long passages of time last – for some find it difficult to understand the concept of ten minutes or half an hour. The sand running out gives a visual warning and this helps them be ready in time, saving last-minute hassles!

Not all children have the same number or severity of difficulties, so not all of these strategies will be needed – it also may be possible to discard some quite quickly and this can give a real sense of progression. The checklists make sure all the difficulties are recognised, perhaps by brothers or sisters who can become impatient, and so they are first line attempts to see what can be done:

- to develop the child's independence;
- to save nagging the child to 'hurry up';
- to save some of the repetition which can be harrowing for all of the family.

Is it ever too late for intervention to make a difference?

There are different times in the developmental process when periods of increased myelination in the nervous system give youngsters another chance to catch up. These are in the first year of life, at ages 1–3, 6½–8 years, at puberty and again in the mid twenties. At the same time the brain jettisons redundant pathways and allows cells to die so that connections between useful pathways can be strengthened (Winston 2004).

So the answer to that important question is a resounding 'no' … although this has to be qualified by saying that taking adolescents back to practising basic movement patterns can be problematic. On the one hand asking a teenager to crawl could be met with scepticism and a 'don't want to try' attitude even when the benefits of repeated correct practice are explained, so practitioners have to think up strategies, e.g. playing crab football where crawling is disguised in a game, or having a turn on the climbing frame or the climbing wall. Then one hand is followed by the foot on the other side. This provides the same action as the cross-lateral crawling skill.

On the other hand teenagers are responsible enough to listen to explanations of what the cross-lateral pattern involves and to try it out, in private if necessary. Once they have mastered the pattern perhaps they could teach it to younger children thus reinforcing it for themselves? The practitioners can support the youngsters by being positive and encouraging, and through taking time to understand just how difficult crawling can be.

NB A dog can be a wonderful source of comfort when 'nobody else understands'. I'm sure parents will say, 'I've enough to do without a dog', but the dog will listen to secrets and hurts that can't be revealed to anyone else; won't object to being cried on; won't make judgments when things go wrong and will always know the way home. And of course the child with dyspraxia can be given the responsibility of looking out for the dog and 'being in charge', which can be a novel and uplifting experience. A dog can even guard a child when he has to be left alone.

Checklists

On the charts, items can be covered with plastic and have Blu Tack or Velcro for fixing to or detaching from a board. Then they can be re-used or moved around when the routine changes as appropriate.

Chapter 2

Studying dyspraxia within a developmental framework

The study of dyspraxia and that of child development complement each other naturally. The patterns of developmental change are the same for all children in every culture, although the rate at which they pass through the stages and their ultimate level of 'achievement', be that motor, social, emotional or intellectual, is different. This means that developmental norms, i.e. the set of statistics which show what 'normal' expectations of children at different ages are, can be set and the achievements of children with dyspraxia can be compared to them, thus giving a reliable way of estimating the impact which dyspraxia has. This gives a clearer picture than the 'hunch' that something is wrong. Dividing the study of development into separate aspects is somewhat artificial because progress, or indeed regression, in one aspect impinges on all of the others; however it is helpful to have a structure that can make this complex study more manageable! The one suggested here (see Figure 2.1), is to subdivide the study of development into four aspects, namely:

1   social development – or the study of how children build relationships and learn to interact in groups;
2   perceptual-motor development – or the study of how children learn to move efficiently and effectively in different environments. This involves using the senses effectively to guide the action;
3   intellectual development – or the study of how children learn to be logical and rational thinkers; how they come to understand the rules and make moral judgments;

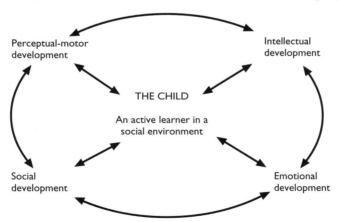

Figure 2.1 The interplay of different aspects of development

4   emotional development – or the study of how children's feelings and perceptions affect their behaviour and learning and how they treat others. This is vital in developing coping strategies if bullying occurs.

Of course, all children are active in constructing the different ways they react to environmental benefits and pressures. This makes the study fascinating, difficult and often unpredictable! Personality factors affect the way different children respond. Some young people overcome huge disadvantages to have happy, fulfilled lives, while others, with apparently much more going for them, succumb at the first hurdle and achieve much less than their circumstances would seem to predict. This is the same for children with dyspraxia. Children with the same level of difficulty react differently. Resilient children will see more opportunities, make the most of them and cope, while more vulnerable children will need a great deal of support for a longer period of time. Still, whether children have a specific difficulty or not, changes in one aspect of development, e.g. through growth or intellectual development or changing family circumstances, impinge on all of the others and the total picture can only emerge when all of these interactions have been considered.

Example

The interactive nature of all aspects of development

After a long struggle Tom learned to swim. Both Tom and all his family were delighted by his progress. But what had he gained?

Well first of all and most obviously, he had taken a huge stride forward, mainly in the perceptual-motor domain, but this progress also spilled over into the other aspects of his development. For now that he was able to swim, he could stay with his friends in the pool, participate in swimming games and talk about Olympic swimmers or local swimming clubs with them. This was an important social gain that would hopefully give him the confidence to build relationships with these *same* children in different settings. And as Tom gained confidence in the water, he was probably interested to discover the names of different strokes, where they were best used and the kinds of physical demands that were needed to perform them. This was an intellectual gain. Possibly best of all, Tom had become more confident in his own ability to learn a new skill and this, enhancing his self-esteem, was a vital emotional gain.

It is particularly important to recognise and build on the spin offs and give lots of praise when children with dyspraxia make progress, because their achievement will have taken a great deal of effort. It would also be helpful to point out to the child that he will be able to use this new skill in different settings, maybe by explaining to Tom that he will now be able to swim in the sea and in other swimming pools, for example. Although this may seem over the top, Rush (1997) tells of one child who learned to swim and then asked her teacher, 'Now will you teach me to swim in my pool?' This child had no understanding that her new skill could transfer to a different environment. This very bright and articulate child thought she would have to learn all over again! And so a moment's thought and explanation can help transfer of learning and prevent all sorts of worries.

This is why Figure 2.1 has arrows linking the different subdivisions of development. They are to remind those who observe children, assess their progress and plan learning activities on that basis, that progress in one area is likely to benefit other aspects of development as well. In similar vein, new or unhappy experiences can cause children to regress to an earlier developmental stage, and then they will appear unable to do something that they had mastered before. This explains why parents can be flummoxed to find that their five-year-old youngster, successfully toilet-trained for some considerable time, has been having accidents in his new school. Perhaps the child has forgotten where the toilets are (did anyone show him?) or stiff new buttonholes defeated fumbling fingers, or the child, unsure of attempting a first-time visit, simply waited for too long before going to the toilet at all. Once confidence is regained through simple but appropriate measures being taken (elastic instead of buttons, clear directions to the toilet with a large red arrow as a reminder, even asking the children, 'Who wants to go?' at regular intervals) some of the problems can disappear!

Even at the top of the school, some children, particularly those with dyspraxia, can find new experiences daunting. Outings from home or from school can cause panic because a whole set of possible disasters loom. 'Treats' such as a class outing, which other children anticipate with joy, mean uncertainty and breaks in a safe routine and appear full of new and unwelcome challenges: 'Where will we go? How long will the journey take? What is going to happen?' There are many 'what ifs', which translate into lots of worries. If the children have difficulty in following sequences of instructions, or in recognising time frames, e.g. how long something takes or lasts, explanations such as, 'We'll go on the bus, then we'll go to the cafe for lunch, then I'll tell you about the afternoon', and reassurances, e.g. that the information desk where the children are to meet after their free time is clearly sign posted as are the toilets, can prevent the children being fearful of losing sight of the teacher and help them to relax and enjoy their day. Some children will also need to know that 'We won't leave till everyone is back', if free time is part of the plan. If this doesn't happen and if the plans are too confusing, children may realise they can't cope and resort to bad behaviour or having a sore tummy – anything that means they don't have to participate. Those who don't understand the children's fears will see only the avoidance tactics, but if the children don't take part, they miss all the learning, both intellectual and social, their vulnerability is exposed to all their peers and this may result in them being ridiculed. Sadly, bullying happens quite often when children and young people have dyspraxia.

What can be done to help?

Rehearsing what will happen is often helpful, especially when boundaries or safety strategies are to be explained. The children could be very relieved to know that 'No one will be allowed to go far from the teachers', or that paths or streets are easy to follow. Those in charge must decentre, i.e. put themselves in the place of fearful children and try to anticipate the kinds of worries they will have.

Recording observations and assessments

As the different aspects of development interact, often in quite subtle ways, it can be difficult to know where to record different assessments. In my view, considering progress across the spectrum and weighing up all the advantages is more important than worrying about recording observations in the 'correct' place. In fact, different viewpoints can form the basis of rich discussions about the children's progress.

Example

Recording accurately

If a child is able to get dressed after PE in an acceptable amount of time now (where previously that was really difficult), what kind of progress is that? Is it intellectual? (The child can now understand the order of putting clothes on and gauge the time to be spent on each action.) Is it perceptual-motor? (The child has now developed the coordination to be able to do up buttons and tie laces.) Or is it emotional? (The child has gained confidence from not being last.) Of course all aspects are important but spelling out the gains to children who exhibit difficulties alerts them to the progress they have made across the board.

The children themselves may put greatest value on the less obvious benefits, e.g. 'When I can swim, I'll be allowed to go to the pool on my own!' Craig is anxious to be independent and free – and when he can manage to do this, he will have made a huge social and emotional step forward. But success will depend on intellectual and motor competence too, for the child will have to remember 'what bus' and how to cope in the dressing rooms, where to find the wristband and how to put it on. Thinking through the organisation of going swimming makes us realise just what a complex task it is.

A more detailed look at the rationale for choosing these aspects of development as key contributors to learning now follows.

Social development

Many parents and teachers would say that the social dimension of learning is the most important one, because if children are happy in school, they are likely to be more receptive and confident and therefore more able to take new learning on board – or at least they will not be afraid to ask for help. Moreover, sociable children are able to interact and learn from their peer group as well as from their parents and teachers. Many important researchers emphasise the importance of active children learning in a social setting. Vygotsky's (1978) concept of 'the zone of proximal development' and Bruner's (1966) idea of 'scaffolding' both claim that if children are supported by more knowledgeable others as they learn, and these need only be one step ahead, as the peer group are likely to be, they will be able to move forward more quickly than if they tried to learn alone.

Social development is therefore vitally important as it enables children to:

- build relationships with others;
- learn from others;
- interact appropriately with adults and children;
- cooperate in group situations;
- take the lead role in decision making;
- take the subsidiary role at appropriate times;
- become aware that others have needs too;
- learn to empathise, i.e. understand different perspectives;

- understand how events affect others;
- develop socially acceptable behaviour in different circumstances;
- make decisions (social and/or moral) and stay with them;
- appreciate the value of friendship; and
- develop altruism, i.e. caring for others at some cost to oneself.

The list, however, shows where children with dyspraxia find it difficult, even impossible to comply, for they often find it very difficult to build relationships beyond the family group. This is not really surprising given that these others are not likely to recognise their difficulties. Or perhaps their difficulties in social situations spring from a general lack of confidence in their own ability to tackle new things and possibly lay themselves open to further disappointment and so they stay close to those they know will offer support. Another social difficulty comes from an inherent block in being able to empathise with others. Some youngsters with dyspraxia seem unable to appreciate another person's success or realise that they are unhappy. Perhaps this is because they have to concentrate so hard on overcoming their own difficulties, or perhaps they don't want to 'look outwards and see' because then they realise that others are managing better than they are – at least in movement tasks. Giving lots of (deserved) praise in activities such as oral story telling or computer work or mathematical reasoning, i.e. in whatever these children do well, will hopefully boost their egos so that they can accept their limitations and cooperate in trying to overcome them. Again this is a case of one kind of progress helping another.

Perceptual-motor development

The perceptual-motor aspects of development concern the acquisition of practical skills through developing abilities such as coordination, balance, control, strength and speed of movement. The underlying skills of planning movements so that they are efficient and effective, involve much perceptual learning based on making spatial and kinaesthetic decisions. These depend on the integration of the senses. These are the vestibular sense or sense of balance, the visual (seeing) sense, the auditory (hearing) sense, the tactile (feeling) sense and the senses of taste and smell. Two less well-known but fundamentally important senses are the proprioceptive (receptors all over our bodies and in the muscles and joints relay positional information when the body is still) and the kinaesthetic sense that provides us with spatial information, e.g. letting us sense directions and distances without looking. All the senses work together to interpret environmental cues accurately. Thus perceptual input into the sensory system correctly guides decisions about when to move, what to move and where to go.

Example

Crawling using the cross-lateral pattern

Let's find how acquisition of one of the early movement patterns impacts on the different aspects of development. Let's look at crawling, usually a favourite way of getting around at about nine months of age. This is an important stage in development, yet parents not understanding the inherent learning within crawling can be pleased when this stage is missed out. But why should it be missed? The strange thing is that children who don't crawl, very often can't crawl. As a result they lack early sequencing and coordination practice, and experience in stretching forward and making spatial decisions, such as how far and in which direction something out there is, while they are in a secure, balanced position. Picture a child in a prone kneeling position, ready to crawl. Imagine one hand stretching forward to go into the movement. As this happens, the body weight must shift to be completely supported by the other three points. This is good practice for learning to balance. If children don't experience this, they are missing out a fundamental stage in learning to move effectively in different environments, for balance is essential to stability both in stillness and in movement, i.e. in being able to stand well balanced and secure with postural control (static balance), and with the body held steady with equal strength on both sides of the body in a forward roll (dynamic balance).

It is interesting and informative to discover that many children who haven't crawled have reading difficulties, sometimes dyslexia *and very often handwriting problems*. One reason is because they have missed out on sequencing practice, i.e. moving limbs in the correct order and so imprinting a pattern of sequential movement into the brain. But most often, not being able to crawl is an early sign of dyspraxia.

Another example comes when children learn to ride a bike – a skill children with dyspraxia find incredibly difficult if they ever master it at all. First the achievement brings a surge in confidence, an emotional gain. Then their social development is enhanced because they can join their friends and travel further from zealous parents! And at the same time they are learning about the timing of the action (when to push), the balance they need, how much strength they need to cope on rocky outcrops and how to steer in particular directions. All aspects of learning are enhanced.

It is vital that due attention and time is given to perceptual-motor development because children demonstrate what they have learned by being able to do something they haven't managed before. A poor demonstration could confuse any assessment, because intellectually there may be no difficulty. So perceptual-motor efficiency enables children to:

- control their movements with increasing dexterity;
- move effectively and safely in different environments;
- develop spatial and kinaesthetic awareness;
- develop the abilities that underlie skilled performance, i.e. balance, coordination and control;
- know how to organise sequences of movement;
- become involved in health giving activities;
- enjoy participating in sports, gymnastics and dance;
- be confident in tackling new movement challenges; and
- show what they have learned.

This is the aspect of development that youngsters with dyspraxia find particularly challenging and many heartrending stories are told when children aren't allowed to play. 'I want to try to play football', cried David, 'but they'll only let me be a goal post – for 45 minutes too – it's not fair.' And indeed, it isn't fair at all. The natural thing is for children to avoid situations like this, for not all children would be as forceful as David was – and of course being left out prevents them having the very practice they require. However, the pros and cons must be carefully weighed up, and if a vulnerable child is being made unhappy, then a substitute activity or a specially designed perceptual-motor programme is the child's right. Examples of activities and programmes are in Chapter 9 and in the appendices of this book.

Intellectual development

Goddard Blythe (2005:5) shows how movement is an integral part of life at every stage. She explains that 'learning is not just about reading, writing and maths. These are higher abilities that are built upon integrity of the relationship between brain and body.'

The intellectual or cognitive aspects of development concern the acquisition of knowledge and understanding about all aspects of everyday life and in all areas of the curriculum. Children need to develop this so that they can learn to:

- develop knowledge and understanding of the world;
- develop language and communication skills;
- develop the capacity to think logically and rationally;
- make informed decisions;
- develop mathematical and scientific concepts;
- solve problems;
- think creatively about new ways of doing things;
- concentrate on the task at hand; and
- cope with specialised learning in the classroom and at home.

All these accomplishments have to be analysed in terms of the underlying movement skills if difficulties in carrying them out arise.

This last item concerns the classroom. Children with dyspraxia are bright and have little trouble with intellectual tasks, however when learning has to be demonstrated through some kind of movement, then difficulties may become apparent. The technical aspects of writing may be problematic due to poor control of the pencil. The tendency to scribe letters back to front due to poor laterality is common in the early years but when it persists beyond age eight then the difficulty merits further investigation.

A short-term memory problem may cause children to forget how the letters are formed. Sequencing difficulties may hamper storytelling as retaining the order of the tale – knowing that the beginning or introduction comes before the middle or main input and that the story must logically progress to the end – is quite taxing. Dyspraxic children often have marked success with oral work because then they can give their imaginations full play and/or solve problems which take quite sophisticated reasoning although writing them down just couldn't happen. Perhaps they could tape-record their stories and transcribe them later? The benefit of this is that the tape can be replayed and paused and this takes away the strain of memorising the story and so it can be written, part-by-part, on different days.

If children with dyspraxia have aspects of dyslexia, and 50 per cent of them do, reading will be problematic and this can confuse teachers into thinking that the underlying concepts of the lesson have not been understood. Using simple words to convey instructions or substituting symbols or pictures for text can be very helpful, depending on the age of the children. The computer is a great boon as children can record their stories, even in conjunction with an audiotape, and then the spell checker can help to reduce mistakes and enhance the chance of success.

In all parts of the curriculum, it is important that the lessons are prepared to take account of the individual children's difficulties and although this is time consuming at the start, soon the rewards for both children and teachers outweigh the time spent. In music lessons, for example, children can be encouraged to select an instrument to match their capabilities – something sturdy like an Orff Xylophone would suit a child who has difficulty gauging the strength needed to play with any kind of finesse. Like the computer, the child can master playing the xylophone, because hands can stay on their own side of the body. Once the child gains confidence, then crossing the midline and more delicate playing can be encouraged. A moment's sympathetic planning can spare a child the humiliation of breaking an instrument and possibly having to endure the jeers of his classmates.

Emotional development

This is perhaps the most difficult area to understand, possibly because the development of confidence, or a *raised self-esteem* is only apparent in carrying out another task or perhaps in changed non-verbal behaviour, for example the gait, i.e. the carriage and the poise in walking. Non-verbal behaviour is always difficult to assess accurately as facial expressions can be very misleading, although lots of teachers will claim to know what is going on inside a child's head. 'I'd be a funny kind of teacher if I couldn't tell if he was trying or not,' said one teacher, but personally I'm never so sure! Often involving the children's own spoken evaluations is a safer bet. Other things like appreciation or imagination are less tangible than getting a sum right and making progress in mathematics, and this makes assessment problematic, but this is a hugely important aspect of development for it allows children to:

- approach new situations with confidence;
- express feelings and emotions;
- cope with anxieties and be more resilient;
- enjoy open-ended problems;
- appreciate works of art/music/dance;
- cry if they want to;
- understand the perception of other people;
- develop altruism;
- pretend to be someone else;
- appreciate the atmosphere, e.g. in a church;
- be innovative and imaginative.

Again aspects of this can be difficult for children with dyspraxia who don't decentre, in that they don't readily understand the perceptions or standpoints of others or their points of view. This makes it difficult for children to play together. Observers must distinguish between children playing in parallel, i.e. two children playing alongside each other but with no common purpose and no interaction, and play where the children act together to devolve some imaginative ploy or build a model or discuss plans.

But why should these children have this problem? Many children with dyspraxia often can't read other children's non-verbal signals and so they make inappropriate responses such as laughing loudly when the game needs them to be quiet. And because they find judging distances difficult, they tend to intrude into another child's personal space. The other child can feel threatened by this, and especially if it happens with a bang and a clatter (due to lack of judgment in how much speed to use), they shy away. The dyspraxic child immediately feels rejected and hurt, without knowing how he offended.

Linked to the difficulty in following instructions, the children with dyspraxia often find it difficult to follow the rules of a game. So many childhood games have unwritten 'rules' and it is difficult for parents to understand what is going on and therefore impossible to rehearse them with their child. But the other children know these rules, seemingly without any explanation, and the dyspraxic child, not understanding, infringes them and is blamed for spoiling the game.

Example 1

Being bound by routine

Listen to Irene, Paul's mum. She explained: 'When Paul developed this great interest in his train set, I was so relieved and I thought, "now is the time to ask two other boys in his class to tea". I thought that if they got to know Paul at home and had a nice time, then at school they would let him play. Before the boys arrived, Paul and I talked about sharing and taking turns and that was fine. On reflection, however, I realised that he had rehearsed what would happen too much. At first all was well, but when the boys wanted to change the route the trains ran and so alter the game, Paul couldn't cope. He got agitated and shouted, "They're not playing the right way – they've got to go home." So they did. Later, when we had calmed down, I realised that was what I often said to Paul, "If you aren't good, we'll have to go home." '

Obviously distressed, Irene asked, 'How do you explain all the nuances of social behaviour to a child with dyspraxia?'

Another difficulty arises if the child takes every utterance, every plan, and every story literally.

Example 2

Difficulty adapting to changing circumstances

Colin explained: 'We have to be so careful how we tell Jake about things we might do. One year we had promised that when we went on holiday he could swim in the sea. When we arrived at St Andrews, the mist was well in over the sea and the beach was deserted, but Jake couldn't be persuaded to wait. "You promised, you promised," he yelled and we had to let him bathe. He couldn't understand that he'd have a better time later when the sun came through. It had to be now because he had interpreted "When we go on holiday" as "the very minute we arrive!" Jake can't cope with any change in plan. Everything has to be done by the book!'

Example 3

Lively imaginations

Leah's teacher spoke about her wonderful stories and her enjoyment of any time when creative thinking was to be shared. While this was a real bonus for Leah and the class, she was also very concerned about the level of Leah's immersion in her fantasy world. 'When she tells about being a fairy, she becomes one', the teacher explained – 'in the garden she tries to eat leaves and berries because that's what fairies eat, and she would jump out of an upstairs window if she had the chance, because that's what fairies do!' And so her parents and her teacher had constantly to watch in case the child was hurt. 'Hannah loves to dream', the teacher explained, 'and sometimes it's quite a thought to pull her back to a harsher world'.

This gives another insight into the thinking of a child with dyspraxia and helps explain the never ending and often perplexing responsibilities that parents and teachers have in keeping their children safe.

Coping with children with dyspraxia is challenging and complex, made even more difficult by the fact that the children at the centre of it all are not passive recipients, but people who make decisions and react to teaching and other forms of intervention in their own way. The Scottish Consultative Council on the Curriculum (1999) agrees, explaining that:

> Each child is an unique individual. Each brings a different life story to the school setting. Growing up as a member of a family and community with unique ways of understanding the world creates an individual pattern and pace of development.

The Early Years' Foundation document in England (2008) similarly stresses the unique nature of each individual child.

And so children bring their own richness to learning through sharing their experiences and interests. Generally speaking, they are greatly influenced by their family's attitude to education; after all, parents are the children's first educators; they are the ones who provide the early experiences and the early cultural impact. And as learning is eased if the children can build on something that is familiar to them, those who teach have to recognise and respect the children's previous learning, their cultural environment and the quality and quantity of the opportunities they have had. Then there is their genetic endowment which plays an important part, for some children will have a greater capacity to do well in school terms, than others. But of course ability alone does not ensure success and less able children are often able to work hard and shine. All the genetic and environmental influences work together to give each child a unique profile. The contribution of each has long been debated. The conclusion has usually been that a constant and complex interplay determines the child's behaviour. Is this different when children have dyspraxia?

Heredity and environment: the interaction when children have dyspraxia

When parents discover that their child has a difficulty such as dyspraxia, they are usually anxious to know 'What has caused this? Is it inherited? Did we do something wrong, perhaps give the wrong food at the wrong time or did we not give enough attention?' The first important point to emphasise is that dyspraxia can happen to anyone and no parent should feel inadequate or guilty. The question of whether dyspraxia is inherited is being investigated to find whether a specific gene can be identified. In the absence of scientific evidence it is interesting to hear what parents say. Parents of children with dyspraxia often endorse the genetic stance. They say, 'Yes, he's just like his uncle', or 'A cousin is having the same kinds of difficulties', or 'She's just like her mum', observations which would seem to point to a genetic source. However, reflection isn't always dependable and if these relations are older than the child, the condition may not have been diagnosed. Dyspraxia may not even have been recognised at that time and so there will be no record more accurate than hearsay! But research is increasingly claiming that dyspraxia is an inherited condition.

In similar vein, and although parents are sometimes nervous about asking, there have been no proven links between difficulties in pregnancy or early attachment problems and subsequent dyspraxia. Yet from the start, some parents know there is something wrong. Perhaps the baby is floppy, with poor muscle tone, or he has difficulty feeding due to the coordination required in sucking or perhaps the baby is tetchy and irritable or a poor sleeper, one who never seems to be at peace. Parents themselves often blame birth trauma, particularly anoxia (deprivation of oxygen to the baby during the birth process) and there are some researchers, e.g. Cotrell (1992), who argue that this *is* the case.

Inherited or not, many parents, worn out by trying to comfort their fractious child, may need outside help for themselves and they can feel so inadequate and disappointed that the relationship with their child is not what they had envisaged. One young mum who had anticipated lots of fun and reciprocal love explained, 'I wanted her to love me. She is all I have, but she didn't, she just cried and cried and when I could take no more, I hit her'. This was an extreme case but many exhausted parents will understand how poverty, a disadvantaged environment and a crying baby just broke the mum down. Parents must be able to get help long before that point is reached for the wellbeing of all the family. A difficult start may also prevent secure bonding, which can have enduring negative effects (Ainsworth, 1972). But of course not all dyspraxic children have early problems, and many families cope very well. Some difficulties don't become apparent until fine motor skills are required. Then parents worry that they have missed early signs. The key thing is for parents to *insist* that they have access to specialist help as soon as difficulties are identified and seem to be more than temporary blips that could be due to the children being off colour, tired or simply uninterested in what is going on.

Does infant feeding make a difference?

A study of the effects of maternal diet on a baby in the first four weeks has been reported by Lucas *et al.* (1992). This showed that for pre-term and small for dates babies, those fed on breast milk showed significant advantages in terms of IQ at age eight. The advantage came from DHA (docoahexanoic), a long chain fatty acid that is beneficial in the maternal diet and for the first four weeks of the baby's life. Ongoing research is concerned with the metabolism of fatty acids and this may show that additions to the diet such as evening primrose oil or fish oil can help some children. Some parents reported immediate improvement in their children's coordination. It is essential, however, that any dietary additions are overseen by the child's doctor as some children react badly to them. Kirby (1999b) explains that children with epilepsy can be made worse, and this may be true for other children as well, so care must be taken until more investigations have been completed.

Goddard Blythe (2008) explains that human breast milk 'carries natural protection through the mother's own immune response'. She points out that breast fed babies are less likely to have ear infections and as the vestibular sense is situated in the ear along with the auditory sense, any infection there may cause a balance difficulty. Breast fed babies also have to work harder to gain the milk and this hard work strengthens the muscles of the tongue and soft palate. This could also help articulation in early speech. Again activity is strengthening the body ready for more challenging actions.

How do parents cope?

Parents' reactions to the diagnosis of dyspraxia are very different. Lots of parents are very distressed because everyone wants their children not to have problems, yet others seem to take it in their stride and say, 'Right, where do we go from here?' Many are relieved to have a specific diagnosis, although some paediatricians can be reluctant to give it. As one parent explained, 'Why worry about giving the child a label? … Surely the label "dyspraxia" is much better than being told your child is lazy, which is what I've been told again and again'. And for those who are Scots, one hugely smiling and totally unconcerned mum told me, 'Och, he's just like his faither, gallus', i.e. very clumsy. The lad seemed to accept his limitations with the same good humour, even though he sometimes 'got clouted for breaking things!' Giving these different examples is intended to comfort parents and reassure them that they are not alone, and to show that there are different ways of reacting, depending possibly on the personality factors of the parents and children, the expectations they have, the resources at their disposal and very importantly, the quality and quantity of help that is at hand.

Perhaps just knowing that there are others who are finding it difficult to cope and offering to meet them to exchange tactics can help; perhaps asking families and friends to give parents a short but regular break can be a life-saver; perhaps even saying, 'It will be better when there are more choices for the child so that his difficulties are not always on display', can help too. A most important move is to build the kind of relationship with the teacher that allows parents to explain in a calm way the difficulties the child has and to suggest ways in which he could be helped. If these can be coping ways in the first instance, the teachers are more likely to welcome suggestions for teaching ways later. Concentrating on the things the child can do, not what siblings could do at the same age, and constantly and consistently praising all the children in the family is the best way. Teachers are always advised to 'catch them being good and praise them'. It's a maxim that rarely fails. As a last resort parents need to remember that there are children who are much more severely disabled. This in no way detracts from the difficulties dyspraxic children have, but it does help to keep them in proportion. (Lists of support groups are in Appendix 5.)

And of course the question of whether the parents have enough information to be able to judge how they should react is important too. Many parents complain that no one has explained what they can do to relieve their children's difficulties. Perhaps this is because of the complexity of the different possible problems which are not evident in every child or perhaps it is because of the difficulty of making prognoses about how different children will develop and to what extent they require support. Children can surprise by how much they can achieve and this is as true of children with dyspraxia as any other, although progress may take longer and need more effort on everyone's part. Very often, short spells of regular practice can give amazing results, but parents and teachers have to be sensitive as to the best time, i.e. not when the children are too tired or interested in something else, for that is self-defeating. Finding something the child wants to be absorbed in and then having short regular private practices until the child feels confident to 'go public' and give everyone a surprise, is often a good way forward!

The question of how parents react to their children's difficulties will obviously affect how the children cope and this brings in the question of environmental influences. All children need lots of love and support but the children with dyspraxia who tend to be isolates or those with a low self-esteem need their security reinforced more than the others. Unfortunately, they can vent their frustrations on the very ones who are helping them most and this causes great distress to the parents and to the children themselves who know that this is the worst thing they can do, but can't stop or plan a better way of behaving.

Example

Frustration making children explode at home

One dad explained what it was like living with ten-year-old Graeme: 'Eventually, I got totally exasperated by Graeme's tantrums and bursts of rage so I went to our GP and explained that although Graeme was doing a bit better socially at school, for his teachers considered him a quiet considerate lad, at home living with him was grim. The doctor said that his behaviour was a compliment to us because he knew we would stand by him no matter what – he felt that his home was a secure place to release his frustrations. What could I say? And we wouldn't have considered drugs, not that they were offered, so it looks as if we'll just have to soldier on and be thankful that school life is a bit more manageable for him. But every day we are anticipating him being angry or sad. It's not easy when our efforts seem to be thrown back in our faces!'

The process of getting enough help and external specialist support is important and one which causes much relief or much anguish. At school, some children have a computer, an auxiliary and a daily perceptual-motor programme while others have much less support, sometimes none at all. One child was given an electric typewriter that had a tiny screen. This meant he could not see what he had written beyond the few visible words and so his sentence structure didn't make any kind of sense. The keyboard was also too small to allow him to type with any degree of accuracy and the frustrations caused by the 'help' were unbearable and unnecessary. The practitioner's response to the agitated parent was, 'But he's bright – he'll manage, I have others who need much more help.' And while we all understand the huge pressures teachers have, this kind of justification doesn't help the youngsters with dyspraxia or the family to cope.

Personality and temperament

One aspect of development, which is claimed to be inherited, is temperament. Children seem to inherit temperamental traits that affect all aspects of their behaviour. Three sets which are particularly applicable to children with dyspraxia are: impulsiveness → reflection and vulnerability → resilience. Doubters might ask how researchers can be sure, given that from the moment they are born, children have role models in their parents. They ask, 'Do children not just copy what they see?' Evidence for the 'nature against nurture' claim is that two children brought up by the same parents in the same environment can be 'chalk and cheese'! One might be quicksilver, acting before thinking and landing in all sorts of scrapes (the impulsive one), while the other child is reflective, carefully weighing up the consequences of doing something and making a considered decision before acting at all.

Then there is the child who is sensitive and easily hurt. Possibly he is the child who gets bullied because he retreats from any confrontation. He is the vulnerable one. His brother, however, shrugs off barbs and arrows and lives to fight another day. Resilient children like this usually have an easier time of it in everyday dealings and they also tend to see and grasp opportunities that pass the less confident child by. Certainly the sunny-natured child appears to have long-lasting advantages over the more sombre one. Garmezy (1993) explains, saying 'Vulnerable children are open to the worst stresses of childhood while others (i.e. the resilient ones) are buffeted from the worst consequences'. Some children always see the bucket as half empty and become distressed while others see it as half full and celebrate!

But if these traits are inherited, what happens if the child inherits 'shyness' from one parent and 'outgoingness' from the other? What then? Bee (1999) explains that typically one gene will be dominant and this will influence the child's behaviour while the other is recessive and will have no effect. However, the recessive gene may emerge again in a later generation. Hence the comment, 'He's just Grandpa all over again!' These temperamental traits, however, are open to environmental modification.

Example

The implications of having different temperamental traits

If a child inherits the temperamental trait 'impulsiveness' and so tends to act without considering the consequences, then a home and school setting which models 'slowing down' and thinking through the outcomes of actions could be salutary. If, for example, adults help the impulsive children practise 'crossing the road drill', repeatedly and calmly pointing out the dangers, then later they may be less likely to dive into the road. Of course, one example won't do much to change usual ways of behaving. Constant and consistent examples are needed to influence temperamental traits that house relatively enduring characteristics. For although children may well learn to slow down in familiar situations, when new ones arise, they tend to instinctively respond in their own temperamental way. Impulsivity does tend to diminish somewhat as children mature – this can be seen when they require less supervision and become more independent. Children with dyspraxia, however, often retain a high level of impulsivity so no one can take any chances that they will be safe. They need extended supervision and this can place a strain on everyone concerned!

Growth and maturation

Although these two terms are often used interchangeably, they are qualitatively different. 'Growth' is a description of quantitive change. The word is most often used to refer to physical growth, but it is really quite a wide term encompassing things like growing vocabulary, growth in skill, in dexterity or logical thinking, growing responsibility or growing independence.

It is fascinating to note that all children in all cultures pass through the same patterns of change although the rate is different, for growth spurts can happen early or late, often causing anguish to the children who fear that they might never happen at all! The timing for most children provides developmental norms that are rough guides to assessment. Physical development is cephalocaudal (i.e. progressing from head to toe), and proximodistal, (i.e. progressing from the centre to the periphery). This is why babies can hold their heads up before their back muscles are strong enough to let them sit and why they can sit before they are able to pull up to stand. Most children crawl, even up stairs, before they walk, for crawling and climbing depend on the same type of coordinated action! The instructions for these sequences are built in at the moment of conception, they are not taught. Even anxious parents can't teach their children to walk. They won't walk till they are 'ready', till they have the strength and balance and coordination, i.e. the maturity, to allow them to try. The fact that most children walk between 11 and 18 months establishes one detail in a timetable of age-norms and this is often used as an assessment device to measure progress. It must be remembered, however, that the span of 'normal' development is wide.

Physical growth in youngsters with dyspraxia is no different to the pattern that other children follow; they are just as tall and their body parts are all in proportion. They meet the growth norms, or size expectations set by chronological age. The children with poor muscle tone, however, will lack strength and this prevents them being able to match the norm in tasks like writing, which is often messy and difficult to read. Lack of strength in the shoulders and/or fingers results in poor pencil control. Nor are they able to kick a ball if the lack of strength is in the pelvic region and legs, for this affects stability and balance and possibly mobility. This means that the children are not able to do the movement skills expected of them by their families, teachers and peer group. They do not meet the expectations indicated by their appearance. And because children in particular value physical prowess highly, and because the demonstration of any movement is public, the children who 'can't do' have a miserable experience which impacts negatively on their self-esteem.

Verbal or oral dyspraxia

When children have poor muscle tone in the mouth it affects coordination in the speech apparatus. They are said to have verbal dyspraxia. Usually they are very late in developing speech although they understand everything that is said. Monosyllabic babbling is late or doesn't develop at all and the children may offer no comprehensible words till they are three years old or so. They then stay with single words for a considerable time. Poor coordination of the lips, soft palate and tongue makes articulation difficult. Speech can be incomprehensible. It can be very distressing for the child not to be understood although sometimes other children can communicate when adults fail. For older children, speaking in front of their peer group becomes impossible, the children stay mute and this can confuse teachers into thinking that their vocabulary is slow to develop. Given speech therapy to help with articulation and then time and encouragement to build up confidence, these children can demonstrate that they have a comprehensive, even imaginative repertoire of words. Parents often need to help a new teacher understand this, for after all they will have 30 or so other children, all with their own sets of difficulties and demands.

Signs of verbal dyspraxia include:

- difficulty in making speech sounds;
- difficulty in ordering sounds to make words;
- difficulty in sustaining the quality of produced speech; and
- difficulty in controlling the rhythm and loudness of speech.

This is quite different from 'selective mutism,' a condition where children can speak clearly at home but not in school or other unfamiliar/stressful situations.

The fact that dyspraxic children are likely to be just as tall and well built as the others may have one disadvantage and that is due, once more, to teachers' expectations of children who are big. Research, e.g. by Lerner (2005), shows that teachers tend to expect big children to cope in a more responsible manner, i.e. they are misled by visual cues, often overlooking the children's chronological age and coping ability. This can negatively affect dyspraxic children who struggle with organisation and planning. They have enough to do to cope with themselves and are not really able to accept more responsibility or look out for others as well. And so there is an important psychological aspect to growth that must be considered.

Maturation

While 'growth' describes the developmental changes that occur over time, 'maturation' explains them. The term means 'the genetically programmed patterns of change which begin at conception and continue till death' (Gessell, 1925). These patterns are inbuilt and untutored. After all, no one teaches a child to laugh or cry or even walk. The effects of neurological and physical maturation can be seen as children become more skilled in coping, i.e. in planning, organising and doing whatever it is they choose to do. This is partly down to the build-up of myelin (see Figure 2.2), a substance that covers and protects the axons in the brain and ensures that messages are transmitted quickly and accurately so that the resultant action is efficient and effective.

There is an important gender difference in maturation. The language centre in boys is myelinated later than in girls and this means that generally they develop language skills slightly later. It also means that while girls are ahead in terms of fine motor skill development, the boys lead the way in spatial orientation tasks such as direction finding and map reading. This does not mean that girls are more intelligent; it simply says that the timing of the acquisition of skills is different due to biological timing. Recognising this is important in setting appropriate tasks at home and in school.

Early motor development

Picture a baby lying in a cot with a mobile just above. The baby is excited to see it, but although she watches it closely, almost without blinking, she makes no movement towards it. In the same situation a month later, the baby can be seen to make a whole range of uncoordinated movements in response to trying to reach it. Facial grimaces show the effort involved but, although arms and legs are flailing, the purpose of the activity, i.e. getting hold of the toy, is not achieved. During that activity, however, the child's hand may strike the toy and gradually she realises that she has some control over her arm. She now knows she can cause things to happen. She is now involved in a problem-solving activity, 'how do I get it to move again?' and after many tries her movements become more refined and accurate until at about four months she can look and reach and grasp, a sophisticated and purposeful set of actions. She has still to work out how to let go – a much more difficult feat! What, then has the child learned?

1   That her actions cause things to happen, i.e. she can be in control.
2   That there is a difference between herself and the object out there. She learns where she ends and the outside world begins, i.e. her body boundary.
3   When to stretch and where to stretch, i.e. how far and in what direction.
4   What happens to the rest of her body when she moves one part.
5   That her successes will be applauded by those watching, i.e. she learns to redo movements which win praise and through that build secure social relationships. This promotes confidence as well as competence in the movement itself.

NB Activity builds myelin.

These are very important developmental gains, primarily in the perceptual-motor field, but confidence in being able to be successful stimulates development in the emotional domain, for those who watch and encourage help her to know that adults will approve her efforts and this enables her to try other things. As the child internalises or habituates a successful movement pattern, she finds that successive 'shots' don't require the same amount of effort. The early thinking and planning as well as the 'learning to do' have been internalised and can be called upon again when a similar movement is required.

The child learns to adapt a learned movement to fit another situation and so a repertoire of increasingly complex actions is built up. Ayres (1972) explains that children with dyspraxia find this adaptation or transfer of learning very difficult. They don't seem to recognise the similarities in patterns and so it takes longer for them to do unaccustomed movements. Through practice they manage habitual movements or everyday movements reasonably well, but new movements can be very difficult; they have to be planned as a first time try. But what kind of maturation allows this to occur? What happens to allow children to develop increasingly skilled movement?

Neurological maturation

The human brain is the size of a coconut weighing about 3 lbs and grey and wrinkled in appearance. It has two hemispheres that are covered by a thin skin of convoluted membrane called the cerebral cortex. Each fold is called a sulcus and each bulge a gyrus. Therein lie the nuclei or thinking cells. The neurons or nerve cells begin to appear about 12 weeks after conception and are all present by about 28 weeks (Figure 2.2). They have an electrical and chemical function that enables them to transmit messages along a one-way connection tube called the axon. A protective coating of myelin to insulate it and protect it from other connective tissue gradually covers this. The neurons are surrounded and nurtured by a vast

Figure 2.2 A neuron

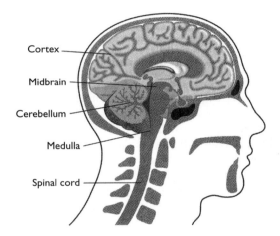

Figure 2.3 The main structures of the brain

number of glial cells. These form the 'glue' that holds the system together. They keep the brain firm and so protect the delicate structures. They also help to remove debris from dying or injured cells. They develop at about 13 weeks after conception and are added till the child is about two years of age.

At the very back of the brain is the cerebellum. It is often called the little brain because it also has two hemispheres. This part is particularly relevant to the study of dyspraxia because it is important in maintaining muscle tone. It also acts as a relay station distributing the sensory input to the correct part of the cortex for analysis.

Each part of the cerebral cortex is divided into four lobes. At the back lies the occipital lobe, made up almost entirely of visual processing areas. The temporal lobe at the side deals with sound and hearing and speech comprehension; the parietal lobe at the top controls movement orientation and some kinds of recognition. And at the front is the frontal lobe, often called the executive centre of the brain because that is the area that analyses problems and makes decisions. Apart from the pineal gland that controls the sleep/wake cycle (Winston, 2004), and which lies deep in the centre of the brain, each part is duplicated in the other half.

If the brain was sliced open, a thick band of fibrous tissue called the corpus collosum would come into view. It joins the two hemispheres, acting as a bridge that transmits instructions from one side to the other so that in effect they act as one (Carter, 2000). Claims are made that a smaller corpus collosum, as is found in boys, can limit the transfer of information. It has been hypothesised that this causes the imbalance in the gender difference between boys and girls (4/5:1) in the numbers presenting with dyspraxia.

At birth the brain stem is developed (Figure 2.3). This carries information from the body to the brain via the spinal column and it responds to 'survival demands' such as hunger and fear. It also regulates basic tasks such as breathing and it sustains blood pressure. It keeps the baby alive. Working upwards the limbic system lies just beneath the corpus collosum. This is the area that generates emotions and the urges that cause us to behave as we do. The thalamus is another relay station directing information to a higher area for processing. The hypothalamus and the pituitary gland work to regulate temperature, constantly adapting it to suit the environment. Children with dyspraxia often are hyper- or hyposensitive to cold and heat. The hippocampus is essential for the long-term memory store and in front of it lies the amygdala where negative emotions are generated.

The least well-developed part is the cortex, the convoluted grey matter that wraps around the midbrain and controls perception, language and movement and all the complex problem-solving scenarios. At birth billions of neurons are present in the cortex but the axons are short and connections between them are not yet made. This explains the helplessness of the newborn infant.

The development of myelin

Each of the modules in the brain has its own function and they are connected by axons, the transmitting bands of the neurons. They are covered by a sheath of myelin, an insulating fibre that protects the axon and allows the message to pass smoothly along it.

In some children, myelination is not complete till age six or so and in some it is still building at adolescence. This can affect children's coordination skills. The timing of this process also helps to explain why paediatricians are reluctant to make early diagnoses of dyspraxia or developmental coordination disorder, for developing myelination may reduce some of the coordination difficulties. It may help to realise that in multiple sclerosis the myelin sheath is breaking down, causing sufferers to lose control of their movements. This is the reverse of the myelination process.

In the cerebral cortex of the brain, millions and millions of these neurons or nerve cells respond to external stimuli from the senses: sight, hearing, smell, touch and kinaesthesis or awareness of where the body is in space.

These neurons have four important parts:

1   a cell body;
2   dendrites or branchlike extensions from the cell body, which are the main receptors of nerve impulses;

3   the axon, which is a tubular extension of the cell body; and
4   terminal fibres at the end of the axon that form the primary transmitting apparatus of the nervous system.

Bee (2007) explains that the branchlike appearance of the dendrites has caused psychologists to use botanical language to describe their function. They talk of the 'dendritic arbor' and 'pruning' of the 'arbor'. What do they mean?

In the embryo, axons are short and there is little development of the dendrites so the connections between the neurons are not yet made. But in the last two months before birth and in the first years after, there is massive activity. The dendritic arbor grows and this provides the vast number of connections necessary for the brain and body to function together. A synapse is the point at which the transmitting fibres from the axon come into close contact with another neuron's dendrites. It is the point where the instructions for action are passed from one neuron to the next. Electrical activity coming from the axon of one neuron releases a chemical, a neurotransmitter, and this stimulates electrical activity in another. This can happen between nerve cells and others such as muscle cells. There are vast numbers of synapses and it is these connections that allow cells to fire together and allow the brain to function efficiently.

This development, however, is not smooth and continuous, for some of the vast number of pathways, which have been formed, are superfluous and by the time the children are three or so, many of the pathways that have not been involved in useful actions will have been pruned. Experience, therefore, does not add new pathways but causes redundant or extra ones to disappear. Unfortunately some good pathways can be pruned and this has been suggested as one reason for the lower IQ in children with Down's syndrome. In mono savants, the special islets of ability that allow prodigious memory (Kim Peake – the inspiration for the film *Rainman*) or superlative artistic skills, e.g. Stephen Wiltshire, is thought to be caused by insufficient pruning.

Think back to the baby in the cot wanting to have the toy, but producing only random, uncoordinated, purposeless movements. At this stage, there are far too many messages being transmitted to all four limbs and these prevent effective movement taking place and only serve to confuse the system. But when successful action is practised, in this case when the child manages to grasp the toy, then the pathways and connections used to achieve that action are reinforced. The redundant ones are eliminated and the wiring diagram is cleaned up (Bee 2004). When the system is pruned like this, information from the senses can be transmitted efficiently because there are fewer unproductive alternatives, fewer choices about where to go!

What then causes dyspraxia?

Following the description of neurological development outlined above, it seems that dyspraxic children have fewer reinforced interconnections and so the cortex remains in a state of immaturity (Portwood, 1998). And so messages that should only go to one limb go to all four. If the child wishes to reach out to lift a cup, then the other arm will stretch forward too, and if the child is asked to walk along a straight line using a tandem, heel to toe walk (an assessment test), his arms will be curled round from his sides without him being aware that this has occurred. These superfluous actions use extra time and energy and may prevent two hands or two feet being used together to do different things, such as holding paper in one hand and cutting with scissors with the other, or standing on one foot and kicking a ball with the other.

Farnham-Diggory (1992) has another suggestion. He explains that:

> A large number of small abnormalities develop during prenatal life, each involving some irregularity in neurone arrangement, e.g. clumps of immature brain cells or congenital tumours. The growing brain compensates for these problems by rewiring around the problem area. These rewirings in turn may scramble normal information processing procedures just enough to make reading or calculation or any specific task very difficult.

Other researchers consider that some children with dyspraxia may have retained some primitive reflexes. These cause involuntary movements, e.g. shrugging, twitching, and fidgeting. They prevent the development of more segmented movements. Blythe (1992) explains this. He claims that, 'The continued presence of a cluster of aberrant reflexes causes writing and copying difficulties, impaired short term memory, the inability to sit still, excessive daydreaming, clumsiness and to a lesser degree mathematical problems' and these are all observed difficulties in dyspraxia.

Like the condition, the answer to 'what is the cause?' is complex. Different researchers have made contributions from their own work which has been undertaken in different environments – schools, hospitals and laboratories – with different numbers of children being assessed in different ways. The children may have been observed doing different everyday coping skills at home or carrying out learning activities in the classroom. If observations are made on several occasions in different environments, e.g. the child in the playground to see if and how relationships with peers develop, or within the home considering how the child copes in the kitchen as distinct from the bedroom where skills of getting dressed are required, then the results *may* be quite different from those obtained by a paediatrician or occupational therapist who has restricted time with the child. On those occasions too, the child may be unnaturally tense in the presence of strangers – especially if he suspects he is going to fail some kind of test or he may be concentrating extremely hard, not a state that could be sustained all day. And so, when reading about research, it is always useful to ask, 'How many children were assessed? What form did the assessment take? How long did the assessment last? What steps were taken to reduce bias in the collection of data, i.e. to assess objectively in the most natural environment?' (Macintyre, 2000b). Whatever the cause, the learning differences that distress children are troublesome and diverse and it goes without saying that they must all be identified and helped.

Labelling

The final discussion in this chapter concerns labelling and it is just as contentious as the issues that have gone before. Certainly a label such as dyspraxia allows parents and teachers to have a common basis for communication, for parents can be increasingly sure that the teachers have at least a working knowledge of the condition. Let's list the points 'for labelling' first.

Labelling is helpful if it:

- lets the children know that difficulties are not their fault. They are not being careless or lazy. They are likely to be trying as hard as they can (Kirby, 1999a);
- gives an accurate indication of what is and what is not wrong;
- allows communication between parents, teachers and therapists;
- means getting support from experts is easier (some authorities insist on a label before providing specialised support);
- allows parents and children to belong to a support group. This *reduces* isolation;
- means that children can meet other children with dyspraxia who know how they feel;
- allows parents to share strategies and helpful ideas, even just let off steam;
- means shared ideas can give everyone confidence in trying new moves; and
- provides the possibility of a disability living allowance to help offset costs.

On the other hand:

- parents and the children themselves may not like the idea;
- there is not a definite cut off point between those that have and those that do not have the condition. The criteria 'significantly interfere with learning' or even just 'not being able to do certain things well' is woolly and unhelpful for borderline children; this is why psychologists make the formal diagnosis;
- the label may suggest an unchanging static picture of difficulties and this is not the case;
- the label suggests a global condition and yet only one or two areas may be problematic;
- as aspects of other conditions blend with dyspraxia, it may be possible to be given the wrong label!

NB Whether they have a label or not, these children can be helped; the label need not stick. Furthermore, the label dyspraxia means that a specific condition is present. This prevents other less supportive labels, e.g. being lazy or clumsy, being carelessly applied.

Chapter 3

Perceptual-motor development

This chapter examines why some young people cannot ride a bike or tie their laces. It studies the underlying abilities as well as offering advice, which would be specific to teaching one particular skill. Despite claims by Cowden and Eason (1991) that 'movement problems may be more difficult to eliminate than other deficiency classifications', it should be stressed that short, regular spells of practice, especially when the children are cooperative and motivated, can make a huge difference. This is just as well, for if children are to be able to cope at home and at school, they must be able to carry out a wide range of activities. They must initiate some action plans and respond appropriately to others, sometimes very quickly. If they have a perceptual difficulty, for example if they take information from the environment incorrectly, they are miscued and the resulting actions are awkward or inappropriate. Or if they 'see what they want to do in their heads but their hands get it all wrong' (Gail's description of her difficulties), or as Donald described his efforts, 'It's like doing jobs with boxing gloves on', they are left confused and frustrated. If there is no help, youngsters can lose confidence and become fearful of tackling movement tasks at all. This leads to lack of practice, which makes the problem worse. There is a further implication, however. French and Lee (1996) write:

> It is widely accepted that the development of controlled movement has a part to play in the intellectual development of children. Children need to experience movement in order to learn about themselves, the relationship to the environment and the interaction of the two.

This shows how important learning to move is. The implications of not moving well spread beyond the movement patterns or skills themselves into the children's intellectual, social and emotional development and particularly affect their self-concept and self-esteem. This 'picture that children build of themselves' influences how they are able to form relationships with others, a critical part of social development. Knowing where they are in relation to outside objects and people out there in the environment allows them to orientate themselves in space so that they are not 'always bumping and getting bruised'. Faulty judgments can cause them to intrude into other people's personal space and this can annoy – not a good way to make friends. This sense is kinaesthetic awareness, which is the first sense to be explained under the heading 'perception'.

Perceptual information comes to the brain through the senses as shown in Figure 3.1.

If children, or adults for that matter, are to move efficiently and effectively, achieving the purpose of the action without extraneous movement, they have to appreciate how their bodies are functioning in the space around them. They have to realise how near they are to

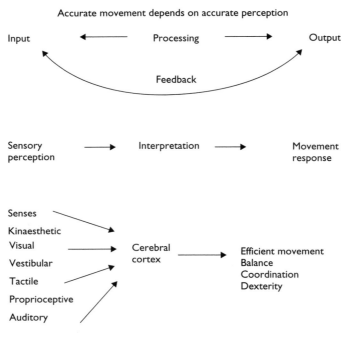

Figure 3.1 The senses and the part they play in moving well

Figure 3.2 Kinaesthetic awareness

other people and objects and gauge the distance between themselves and different things out there in the environment (this is spatial awareness). They have to *sense* where their different body parts are in relation to each other and realise the effect moving one part has on the others (this is body awareness). They also need to know where their bodies end and the outside world begins. This is called body boundary (see Figure 3.2).

The sensory system is part of the nervous system. The sensory receptors take information from the external environment by seeing, hearing, touching, tasting and smelling and from the internal ones, i.e. through the vestibular, proprioceptive and kinaesthetic senses. When efficient, this input works in an integrated way to effect the demonstration of movement.

But before assessments about children's sensory perception and integration are made it is a good idea to check their understanding of directional words.

Ways to practise these words

Practising these words can happen in the classroom or the hall and in the garden, yard or playground when the weather is fine. In the school hall, all sorts of apparatus layouts can help spatial orientation, especially if teachers remember to stress the spatial concepts as the children enjoy the movement. Perhaps the younger children can say the words

Table 3.1 The senses: their function and indicators of diffficulties

The senses	Their key role	Indicators of difficulties
Vestibular	Balance	Unsteadiness, unwilling to leave the ground or take risks
Kinaesthetic	Spatial awareness: primarily when moving	Unable to judge distances, bumping and spilling
Proprioceptive	Body awareness: primarily when the body is at rest	General clumsiness
Visual	Seeing, discriminating and tracking, focusing	Squinting, rubbing eyes, sore eyes, peering, holding a book too close
Auditory	Hearing and listening, discriminating sounds	Distractibility, inability to repeat accurately, delayed acquisition of speech, spelling difficulties
Tactile	Feeling and touching, tolerating being touched	Poor tolerance of rough textures, hates hair and nails being cut
Taste and smell	Accepts/rejects food, smells can overpower, a poor sense of smell can affect the ability to taste	Unwilling to try new foods, upset by strong smells, even perfumes and soap/aftershave, chemical sprays

Table 3.2 Directional words that can confuse children's movement

Simple directions	More complex directions
Up, down, near, far away	Opposite; directly facing
Above, under, below	Beyond, through
Forwards, backwards	Sideways, diagonally
Curving	Swerving round
	At an angle

'through, under, over', as they go and the older ones can try to remember their route and draw it out (mapping skills) when they go back to the class. This also stimulates the short-term memory, which is a major problem for children with dyspraxia. If the children work in groups, the ones with difficulties won't feel so exposed and even if the others do most of the remembering, it doesn't matter, because they are actually helping the children with dyspraxia to recall what went on some time ago in a different setting.

In the classroom, all sorts of 2-D activities such as 'join the dots' with explanations such as 'These dots are near each other so you just need a little line and some are far away so your pencil has to travel a long way', help the younger ones appreciate distances. For the older children 'lost in the circuit' puzzles with questions such as, 'How is the policeman going to catch the convict?' should elicit replies such as, 'Well, he'll have to go forward a short way, then up over the bridge and through the wood. That's a long way'. These simple activities promote awareness of distance, help the children internalise the spatial concepts and also, and very importantly, help planning and organisation. The children have to make decisions about where to go and also think about the order or sequence of events, i.e. do this and then that. If they trace the route with their pencil, then their fine motor control is being practised too. More complex questions can challenge older children, e.g. 'Where will the convict go to escape? Could you plan a better route?' These abstract questions need a much more sophisticated appreciation of the problem.

Perhaps after trying some of the activities above, one group of children could set up a circuit with gym apparatus in the hall or design a treasure map for another group to follow. All activities that help young people with dyspraxia appreciate 'where to go' can be lots of fun for all of the children. The important thing is that parents and teachers recognise the important learning possibilities within simple, everyday games. Hugely complex ideas are not required. An analysis of some old-fashioned favourites to identify the learning possibilities does very well. Even pinning the tail on the donkey (using Blu Tack), involves fine motor skills and spatial awareness – judging distances in a fun way. Who remembers 'In and out the dusky bluebells'? The party game is old-fashioned, but still greatly enjoyed. It could be part of an 'ask Granny project' that often is done to gather stories and artifacts of the Second World War. The idea of a circle of children making arches for some to weave their way 'under and through, moving from back to front' could lead to a more complex parachute game. In this version the children have to lift the parachute twice. On the first lift, the nominated children have to wind through as many arches as they can and on the second they have to dash to the other side. These games help develop spatial concepts as well as laterality, i.e. – awareness of movement at the sides. Body and spatial awareness is also required if the children have to bend far enough to go under the arches.

Dressing the clown – or the cowboy or other characters for the school assembly – can be a useful activity, for this can also help with the organisation of getting dressed at home, which is difficult for some children with dyspraxia. Children of different ages can have fun with this activity. The teacher or the older children produce a simple outline of the character and then the younger ones have to dress him. This can be with actual clothes shapes which they have drawn, or if recognition of shapes (triangles, rectangles, circles, hexagons, etc.) is an appropriate learning focus at this time, the children can stick on circles for buttons, make a bow tie out of triangles, use rectangles for shoes and so on. Again it is helpful if adults can control the pace of the activity so that its purpose is not lost, e.g. What will we put on first? What do we need next? The actual sticking the shapes on to the body helps fine motor control.

Clown

How many steps forwards will you need to reach, Ian? Four? Let's try! How many small steps will you need too get back to the start?

All sorts of variations of this can be used, e.g. drawing round the children themselves to make life-size models and then dressing them up for a disco or going to a wedding, whatever you like! This simple-to-prepare kind of activity can be enjoyed by all of the children in the class; it's not expensive and inherently it houses so many learning skills to do with spatial awareness and body awareness. After the 'models' are complete, the children can explain why they are dressed this way and even use them as a stimulus for a play. Sometimes the children get too enthusiastic and the models get cluttered, so simplicity is the name of the game!

Once the children grasp the concept of distance, they can have fun working on 'how near?' or 'how far?' i.e. challenges that involve estimating distances.

Stories or songs can also develop spatial reckonings, e.g. 'Let's go fly a kite' from *Mary Poppins* can lead to the children making kites and later trying to fly them. Distance words, e.g. beyond, soaring, into the sky, spiralling, all help develop spatial awareness. This kind of activity houses lots of possibilities for science and craft and shape awareness and appreciation of the spatial concept, 'beyond'. This is often a difficult one for many children to grasp, even for those who do not have dyspraxia.

When people mention 'distances' they usually think of quite long ways apart. But children writing stories, as they do at all stages of the primary school, constantly have to judge distances between one word and the next. 'Keep your words nicely spaced out' is a common teachers' cry. The children are sometimes urged to measure the space between words with their finger but this can mean crossing the midline, a task which children with dyspraxia find extremely difficult. If sequencing is difficult, the written page can appear as a jumble of letters, yet the children with dyspraxia are clear about what they want to say. Opportunities for oral reporting or using a computer are often the best ways to try to help, as the amalgam of difficulties outlined above interact to prevent 'good writing' (see Figure 3.3).

Handwriting practice is a very worrying time for children with dyspraxia. Before they begin they know they are not as good as others in the class. Their letter formation is invariably poor and can be in the wrong order due to poor auditory sequencing. Furthermore, the children anticipating a poor result are likely to be tense. 'My brain knows what my hands are to do', explains Grace, 'but they just won't do it. And I can't do it again, because when my hands are tired, it's even worse.'

Figure 3.3 Grace, aged 12, is copying out some information from the dyspraxia foundation to give to her teacher

Repetition is not the answer, for it usually means more failure. Allowing Grace to use the computer and praising her work for the language content or the imaginative ideas is much kinder than worrying her with presentation issues – after all she won't have to write by hand very often in later life. The actual scribing is a less important skill than the ones she can probably do, but if it has to be endured, then making sure the child is well supported on a suitable chair so that she doesn't feel insecure, helping her with the angle of her paper, especially if she is left-handed, and making sure she has enough time in a quiet place are all helpful strategies.

If children have to write a story, then drawing pictures illustrating the sequence of events or cutting them out of magazines gives a visual reminder and often lets children continue without constantly asking, 'what comes next'. This both relieves the teacher and lets the youngster feel independent. It also stops other children and often their parents becoming resentful about the extra support the dyspraxic ones usually require.

Body awareness

It really is quite amazing how much children and adults take for granted. Doing up buttons without looking; tying a bow behind one's back; playing an accordion where the two hands cope with vastly different jobs; folding arms – the intricate uses of the different body parts are endless. But moving them in a coordinated way depends on an accurate sense of where they are in relation to one another and being able to cope when the movement of one part affects the others.

Proprioceptors

Most young people with dyspraxia lack the sense of placement, which proprioceptors should provide. If they want to step up onto a chair, for example, they will look to check where the supporting foot is in relation to the chair – they won't be able to sense its position. This is because their proprioceptors, or nerve endings in the muscles and skin, are not relaying information as they should. Lots of actions are affected. Sitting down without looking involves a judgment of where the body is in relation to the chair and this in turn tells how much strength or release of strength is required to carry out the movement efficiently. A child lifting a cup needs to know where and when to curl his fingers round the handle and how much strength to use so that the liquid does not spill. Those with efficient proprioceptors will manage this easily, almost automatically, but children with difficulty will clutch the cup against their bodies for extra support. They also have to look at the ground closely every step of the way rather than sensing where their feet should go.

Body boundary

If children are sitting together on the carpet in class or lining up in a queue, those with poor proprioceptive feedback will not keep a space between themselves and the other children. They don't realise they are crowding and bumping till it happens and they are scolded by the teacher or the other children push them away. Even more important is the fact that a poor sense of body boundary can affect safety. Children don't realise how close they are to the edge of the kerb or the edge of the swimming pool. Parents and teachers have to constantly watch out for everyday tasks which herald danger for these children. This can be time consuming and wearing for the adults and equally frustrating for the children when they reach the stage of wanting to be independent.

Practices with lightweight small equipment can help. A small wooden bat and a shuttle-cock and a 'beat your own score activity' where the children hit the shuttle in the air is excellent for the sound helps alignment and the dropped shuttlecock is easily retrieved. Dribbling a football round skittles similarly helps spatial awareness, judging distances and foot–eye control.

Anthony is compact in the spinning cone but Michael isn't aware that his foot is trailing over the edge. He needs support in body awareness activities (see Chapter 9) and strengthening work especially for his legs.

So a poor kinaesthetic and proprioceptive sense leads to children:

- having a poor sense of poise e.g. the child who has to slump over the desk (make sure the feet are supported on the floor and that the desk is the correct height);
- being easily tired by the constant effort needed to stay erect;
- constantly moving and fidgeting in an effort to have feedback to help balance; and having,
- having poor depth perception causing stumbling or 'falling over thin air';
- having poor sense of direction (rehearse 'where to go' ahead of the child having to do so independently);
- having poor body awareness (play 'Simon says' types of games).

Tactile sense

This is a most interesting sense and difficulties are perhaps less well understood than in the more obvious ones. There are two aspects to consider. First, some children can't bear to be touched. Even brushing lightly against them can cause them to overreact, sometimes lashing out – to the dismay and surprise of the offending adult or child. Sometimes they can't endure taking hands in a circle, and the other children naturally feel rejected as they don't understand the source of the refusal and take it personally. This same over-sensitivity can cause ructions at hair cutting or nail clipping times as the sensations are felt much more severely than normal. Some children cry with the hurt of it all. Wearing a watch can only be tolerated if the strap is smooth and made of leather – not plastic, as it is more likely to stick to the skin. Some children wear their socks inside out as the seams irritate them all day. This extreme sensitivity can be seen as allergies in some children.

The second touch difficulty comes when children need hard feedback from the environment. The children are asking their proprioceptors to do their job and send them messages that let them orientate themselves in space. These are the children who thump around. Everyone says, 'They don't know their own strength'. A child who is constantly out sharpening his pencil is one – because when he pressed too hard the lead broke! The teacher may see this as an avoidance or disruptive tactic and be cross. Maybe a harder lead pencil or a ball pen could be the answer? Combine this 'too fast and too strong' approach with distance misjudgments, and you can understand why teachers don't give children with dyspraxia the responsible jobs that most children love to have. And of course the child who bumps and clatters can irritate other children too and when toys are broken or precious things are spoiled, patience does run out!

Observation points indicating a poor tactile sense:

- dislike of being touched so withdrawing from contact;
- may be a compulsive toucher;
- pain may not be registered appropriately causing over or under reaction;
- poor temperature control;
- allergies – possibly eczema;
- dislike of contact sports/games;
- if the child lacks protective control, he may not sense danger.

Visual sense

Assessing vision should cover much more than distance vision that is often the main concern in a simple eye test. Children who 'pass' this can still have difficulties tracking, i.e. following the words on a page or the writing on the board. Functional vision depends on maturation of the Central Nervous System.

Visual-motor integration skills are as important as distance sight. The two eyes have to work together to focus on an image (convergence). Some children with poor convergence will see double images that confuse letter recognition; others will see the letters move on the page and may endure severe eyestrain trying to adjust to the movement. This is Mears-Irlen syndrome and can be helped by coloured overlays or coloured lenses in spectacles. Children also benefit from being allowed to choose the colour of paper that suits them best – different colours defeat reflection of light – and from reading non-justified print (for example Barrington Stokes, Publishers).

Children must also be able to adjust their focus so that they can decipher objects and print from different angles and directions. This is called accommodation. The three skills, convergence, accommodation and tracking are all prerequisites for quick identification and reading fluently without strain.

Observation points indicating a poor visual sense:

- poor reading ability due to discrimination/tracking difficulties;
- child explaining that letters jump or overlap on the page;
- rubbing eyes or partially closing them to keep out the light;
- distress at being asked to read;
- difficulty following written work on the board;
- handwriting sloping in different directions;
- poor letter formation.

Tracking

Tracking affects copying from the board. By the time the child has found the correct place on the board and then looked down to a jotter, the place on the board has been lost. Having an inclined desk board can make a big difference, because the transition from vertical to horizontal is reduced.

The vital message from parents, however, is 'cut down the amount of work the children have to do!' Some parents copy all the sums out in jotters for their children and leave the children to fill in the answers. Could classroom assistants do this for children whose parents can't or won't carry out this task? Parents report that reducing the workload in this kind of way has made a tremendous difference because their children can now keep up with the rest of their group. Imagine the positive input to these children's self-esteem. To know you are not going to be last is such a huge relief.

Example

Nadia explained, 'I was always afraid of being last. I dreaded hearing, "Come on Nadia, last again, we haven't got all day, you know". It got to the stage that I spent so much time trying to find out where other people were on the page that I got even further behind. To make matters worse, they thought I was copying! However, now I don't have so many sums to do. I can do the actual sums anyway, I just can't do them fast when there's lots of writing.'

In mathematics, children find it difficult to line up columns of figures and if these are written incorrectly then despite the actual arithmetical function being correct, the answer will always be wrong. The only way forward is for teachers to have the time and opportunity to make an accurate diagnosis of where the child's difficulties lie. If this doesn't happen the teacher will think the child doesn't understand and try to change the teaching method, whereas it's not comprehension but spatial planning that is causing the problem. Accurate assessment is the key. This takes skill and practice, but it is essential if children with dyspraxia are to flourish.

Three-dimensional vision

Another visual difficulty is often having poor three-dimensional vision. If children see objects as flat against the background rather then standing out from it, it is not difficult to understand why bumping and bruising occurs . . . the table is seen as being slightly further away than it really is and approaching it means bumped legs and juice being spilt or clattered down, and in the cloakroom coats don't fix on pegs because the hanging action misses the target! In the classroom, the children with poor perception of depth may not be able to interpret visual aids and they certainly won't appreciate perspective in art classes. Some children can't find their shoes if they lie on a patterned carpet. So both at school and at home plain backgrounds can save time and effort in focusing through complex patterns or hunting for things that are not really lost.

Auditory sense

During the first three years, the child is listening and learning to tune in to sounds of his mother tongue. At three we are all international (Winston, 2004). After that it is harder to adjust to the tenor of another language. Obviously, loss of hearing significantly affects learning, but children who 'can hear' may have auditory discrimination problems and these may be the basis of a recognised additional learning need e.g. dyslexia or dyspraxia. If the child cannot hear the difference between 'p' and 'b' or 'sh' and 'th' then both reading and spelling are impaired. Even silent reading is affected because then the child listens to an inner voice. If the sounds are not clear then this process will be affected just the same as in reading aloud.

Hearing too much, (i.e. auditory hypersensitivity) can cause as much difficulty as not hearing enough. Children bombarded by sound can have difficulty selecting what they need to hear from the variety of different noises around them. Even in a quiet classroom, some children find hearing the teacher difficult, as they cannot cut out minor rustles and squeaks.

Sounds are transmitted to the language-processing centre in the brain. The right ear is the more efficient – sounds heard there pass directly to the main language centre in the left hemisphere whereas left-eared children have to pass the sound to the language sub centre and then through the corpus collosum to the left hemisphere for decoding. This slight delay may put left-eared children at a disadvantage.

Observation points indicating a poor auditory sense:

- easily distracted by sounds that the others ignore;
- over sensitive to sounds seen when children clasp their hands over their ears;
- under sensitive in terms of pitch and tone, e.g. not being able to tell if a note on a piano is high or low;
- confused when trying to distinguish the sounds of different letters. Here a 'look and say' method of teaching reading can be more successful than phonics.
- slow in responding to instructions;
- not hearing questions clearly affecting responses, e.g. hearing 'boating' rather than 'voting';
- constantly asking for things to be repeated;
- copying others rather than hearing the instructions for themselves.

Children who listen well have a good chance of learning well. If hearing is a problem, responses to instructions can be delayed and this causes problems from rising till bedtime. If the children have to concentrate hard to hear clearly – all day long – they just have to have a break and so 'switch off'. When adults say 'He's in a world of his own', this is what they mean. The other world is far too busy. Understanding this, teachers can organise short spells of activity and very quiet times. Some schools have a quiet room, which children from different classes can use. This is wonderful for children with dyspraxia and it gives everyone a break.

Vestibular sense (sense of balance)

The vestibular sense is the leader of the sensory orchestra. It is the first sense to 'work' and even before birth it helps the baby to get into the head down position ready to be born. Many children later found to have dyspraxia have had a c-section or a breech birth. When difficulties became apparent parents often consider that the birth process itself was to blame. Interestingly it could have been that the sense of balance wasn't helping the babies to get into the correct position and this was the difficulty that necessitated intervention.

Vestibular receptors are situated in the inner ear and work to coordinate movements that require balance. This is why children with an ear infection can find they feel off balance. An ear infection can even cause them to feel very sick. Children without innate balance difficulties will not be so severely affected. In fact some may actually search out this sensation of vertigo (almost losing control) by visiting the fairground. There the whirling and spinning causes them to lose and regain balance. Youngsters with dyspraxia hate this feeling of being out of control.

In dyspraxia, the vestibular and proprioceptive senses may not give enough feedback for the children to have an accurate picture of where they are in relation to objects in their environment or how the body parts relate to one another and this can result in the lurching gait and clumsy movements which many such children have. The vestibular sense should initiate responses to changes in the head position, automatically coordinating the head and body.

How to help

Games and activities appropriately structured to the children's specific profile of difficulties are the answer. Why do these need to be devised? Well, teachers in the gym as one example might prepare an activity where two children standing closely back-to-back have to lean against each other to lower into a sitting position. The activity could help children with poor body awareness feel where their backs are, through the pressure exerted by the other child. This could be very useful unless the dyspraxic child was one who could not bear to be touched – one who was extremely sensitive. Then the choice of activity would be very wrong for that child, causing him to be really upset if not harmed. This shows that all teachers who interact with children with additional support needs must be clear about each child's profile and be careful not to intervene unwisely.

There are lots of songs and rhymes for the younger children that do not have this contact problem, e.g. 'Heads, shoulders, knees and toes' – and always adding 'heels, bottoms, backs and nose' to encourage awareness of the back. 'Incy wincy spider', 'Simon says', 'Here is the church, here is the steeple' are other favourite, useful activities.

Types of movement and movement abilities

All of the senses which have been described should work together to help produce movement that is effective and efficient, i.e. which is balanced, in the right direction and using the correct amount of strength and speed so that a rhythm emerges. This saves both time and energy.

There are different kinds of movement depending on the response that is required. Generally, movement patterns can be subdivided into three kinds. These are:

1   gross movements
2   fine movements
3   manipulative skills.

Gross movements

Gross movements use the large muscle groups that work together to produce actions such as walking, running, jumping and climbing. They need a good deal of balance, strength and control, the underlying competences that lead to whole body coordination. These basic movement patterns develop as children mature, although children with dyspraxia will tend to develop them at the later end of the 'normal' time range and will be seen to use more effort than children without this difficulty. While most, but certainly not all children with dyspraxia are rather ungainly, with continued practice they usually do achieve the everyday patterns at a level that allows them to carry out routine tasks and coping skills at an acceptable level of competence.

Fine movements

The demands made by fine movements are different – speaking, eating, writing and playing the piano are examples that show that only small body parts are used. This can be easier for some children, because when one part of the body is 'fixed', as in sitting, it

Playing the piano

does not need to be controlled and full concentration can go to the moving parts. But of course fine movements can be very intricate, involving hand–eye coordination – e.g. cutting food and threading beads, or greater rhythmical awareness, e.g. in playing the piano, or significant control in a small area, e.g. in writing or colouring in. Playing the piano is a very useful activity because the sound gives feedback, indicating the strength that is being used. Short, easy tunes are motivating and hands can be watched as they gain control and, through that, fluency.

These movements also can involve the children in 'crossing the midline of the body' as in drawing a rainbow or reaching across to tie laces on the other foot and this is very often tricky. In fact, finding that children have this difficulty can be one of the key indicators of dyspraxia. Teachers need to note this difficulty carefully in any profile of needs. A related difficulty comes if children have not established hand and foot dominance. This may not happen till children are six years old, but it can cause the children to appear uncoordinated and clumsy when they fumble because they are undecided in which hand or foot to use.

Manipulative skills

This kind of activity requires that the children cope with outside objects such as pencils or bats, knives and forks. To do this they have to cope with added control demands, e.g. holding the swinging bat against the impact of the ball or pressing hard enough to cut their food. They also have to have a developed sense of body boundary – where they end and the object begins. And of course they have to make the object follow a pattern when writing or a trajectory when throwing a ball. This takes practice and can be very difficult if muscle tone is poor. Children with poor shoulder control will find it difficult to control a pencil, especially if they are not sitting at the correct height of table. Having a triangular grip can help children whose pincer grip is not well developed or retained. Retained palmer reflexes mean that the hand will curl round the pencil and this results in an awkward grip that makes writing very difficult for the child and illegible for the reader. But readers have to persevere because wonderful stories can be hidden in a messy text.

Timing of development

In young children, gross movements involving balance and coordination of the large muscle groups are generally developed first. This explains why some children can run yet be unable to control a pencil. And of course children have been practising these kinds of movements longer! This sequence of development also explains why children's difficulties may not be apparent in the earliest stages. Parents can miss fine motor skill difficulties because they assume that because the gross motor skills are achieved, the others, the fine motor skills, will be proficient as well. Some children, however, can carry out fine motor skills well and yet not manage the gross movements in a coordinated way at all. It would be interesting to know what part practice plays in this. For if children fall and get hurt, as they try to run and jump, they are likely to avoid the scenario which caused the pain and so they may prefer to have jigsaws or art work. Practice then brings success and this gives the child positive reinforcement and motivation to continue.

Open and closed skills

When children have difficulty mastering a skill, then simplifying the demands is a good method of support. Many open skills are needed in a game of football, as the technique has to adjust to the terrain, the kind of pass that is required and the speed and technique of the approaching opponent. Taking this back to the stage where the youngsters practise the technique in a simpler or closed environment is the answer. In other words distractors are cut out and the technique can be grooved.

Swimming in a pool is a closed skill because the environment is unchanging but open sea swimming is an open skill if waves and jellyfish and other swimmers add environmental demands. So if children with dyspraxia are unwilling to try new activities, thinking out and reducing the environmental demands can boost confidence. These can gradually be replaced as competence grows.

Assessing movement patterns

Every movement, large or small, has three parts (see Figure 3.4).

When movement is smooth and efficient, the three parts flow together and the momentum from one part carries on to help the next. In sequential movements, the recovery from the first completed movement blends with the preparation for the second. Flowing movement has an inbuilt rhythm and an awareness of this can clarify the pattern, for example where the strong parts need to come, and where strength should be released. Children can be helped to 'listen' for the rhythm, then clap or stamp it out. This is very good for children who have difficulty listening. This mental preparation helps them visualise the planning necessary to carry out a successful movement pattern.

In efficient movement, the preparatory phase 'gets the body ready' by deciding on the speed that will be needed, the direction of travel, the parts of the body to be used and the

Figure 3.4 Analysis of a movement pattern

sequence of the action. Complex movement patterns require a great deal of mental planning and preparation. Think of attempting a long jump or even the triple jump. All of the stride pattern and timing elements have to be mentally rehearsed before the athletes begin to approach the take off point! This is why they take some time contemplating all the demands of the task before setting off. Children attempting tasks such as running and jumping off a bench, challenges which can be just as demanding for them, may have the added difficulty of watching others to ensure that they will not run across their path and spoil their attempt. Children who can't plan ahead, who can't visualise what comes next, have to make on-the-spot decisions and if they are flustered by being rushed they may well make the wrong ones. Similarly, children who can't cut out visual distractors have difficulties because other children running by cause them to lose their concentration. Many children need more time, more help and possibly less challenge if they are to stay safe.

Balance

The most crucial movement ability is balance. It is central to all movement – much more than being able to stand still or adjusting the body weight to allow standing on one leg. This is static balance or postural control and it is important in maintaining poise and posture, but there is also dynamic balance which controls the body as it moves, working perhaps to sustain equilibrium in a jump or in a forward roll or when the body changes direction. If adults wish to assess children's balance, they must observe the child moving and being still.

Children with dyspraxia can find balance difficult and they often have to be helped to adopt positions which help their postural control, e.g. by being supported by a classroom wall when others are sitting without support; by having a frame or handle near the toilet so that they may sit securely; by having their feet supported if their desk is too high for them to have a secure writing position. This is very important, for if the children have to struggle to maintain their balance, they have less energy to concentrate on whatever else needs to be learned.

Vision helps considerably in maintaining balance, and if the dyspraxic child's functional vision isn't good, giving him a point in space to 'fix' his attention on can help. Then he can align his body position with that spot. Mirrors only provide back-to-front cues and can be confusing. Often it's a case of trying different strategies out in a fun, non-threatening way.

Balancing and learning to ride a bike

Nearly all children want to learn to ride a bike. It's a symbol of growing up as well as the means to travel further afield with friends. Children with dyspraxia find this skill very difficult because of the balance, coordination and steering demands and because their cues from the environment may cause them to make faulty judgments, e.g. about distance they are from the edge of the road. Many teachers would say 'Leave teaching this skill till the child's movement abilities have improved', but the trouble is that the children won't wait; they desperately want to ride the bike *now*!

What advice could be offered to help?

First the bike has to be small enough so that the child can place two feet firmly on the ground and the frame has to be sturdy enough to give real support. If not, the control demands may be too great. (There are now bikes without pedals that require the children to push themselves along. This is an easier way of them finding how to balance). Then the child should sit astride the bike and propel himself along a flat, even path for grass tends to be too bumpy or sticky. Once the child is confident that he can keep the bike upright, then move to a gentle slope that flattens out and do the same again. Ask the children not to put their feet on the pedals – rather lift the legs a little way keeping them ready to stop. The bike without pedals saves legs being bumped.

Only when balance is secure should children attempt to use the pedals, for if they try this too soon, the problem of not being able to judge the correct amount of strength means that too much may be applied and the bike will probably tip over or take off at speed. This gives the child a fright and his confidence will take a knock even if his body doesn't! Some children will need to look down to see where their feet are before they can place them on the pedals so adults should offer some physical support at this point. A very gentle slope will provide just enough momentum. There should be enough distance for the bike to travel in a straight line so that there are no steering problems at this stage.

Steering can be difficult. There are so many other things to think about that many children go round in circles. This happens when they lean too heavily on the handlebars so adults must check that the seat is comfortable and at the correct height. Sometimes drawing a circle on paper and explaining what happens if the handle bars are turned too sharply, can help children who learn best through visual cues. Above all, remember how difficult learning to drive was and stay calm as you persevere, for when the child manages to control the bike – and he will, it will be a real cause for celebration and the sense of achievement will do lots to cement a happy relationship.

Speed of movement

This refers to the time taken to react to a stimulus and to move at a chosen and appropriate speed. Understanding the difference between the two can help clarify a child's difficulties and therefore contribute to accurate assessment.

(i) Reaction time (RT) is the term used to describe the time between the perception of a given stimulus and the beginning of the response. Children with quick reaction time tend to do well in competitive activities of short duration, e.g. sprinting, net play in badminton, or in games where instructions are called out and the pupils are required to make an immediate response.

NB Reaction time should not be confused with reflex action, which is purely automatic.

(ii) Movement time (MT) is the time the action takes from beginning to completion.

(iii) Response time (RT + MT) covers both reaction and movement time.

In analysing a poorly carried out action, it is important to keep the two 'times' in mind, for poor performance in one does not necessarily indicate poor performance in the other. Reaction time can be improved by focusing the child's attention firmly on the stimulus and perhaps giving prior warning of any sudden response, e.g. fixing eye contact with the child as you slowly say 'Are you ready?' at the start of a race. Improving the movement time requires analysis of the movement pattern into its preparatory, action and recovery stages, so that appropriate correction may be made as necessary.

Observing and measuring movement

A movement observation checklist is given in Appendix 1. This is to facilitate recording while observing the children as they practise and become ever more effective and efficient movers and hopefully more confident youngsters. For children who are consistently functioning at a level below that of their peers, specific tests to measure their ability in balance, coordination, speed of movement, body awareness, spatial and rhythmic awareness, may be needed. These tests, which are fun to do, have been specifically designed to isolate the faulty component so that effective remediation can then be planned. However, it must be said that test results usually hold no surprises for teachers who have had the opportunity to study their children over time and in different environments. Tests don't claim to do more than measure performance on more than one occasion, and assessors, despite trying to put children at their ease, recognise the stress factors (i.e. new venue, 'strange testers', not knowing the implications of the outcome), which are sure to bias the results. Some regions, however, insist on formal testing before providing access to support. The results also assure parents and professionals that the diagnosis is correct.

Chapter 4

Intellectual development in young people with dyspraxia

As most children with dyspraxia have average or above average intelligence, a chapter on intellectual development may seem superfluous, but just like the optician who says the child can 'see perfectly well' and the audiologist who reports 'no problem with hearing', those who wish to understand their children's learning differences – and given their level of intelligence, these can be surprising – must consider the children's functional intelligence, because it is aspects of that, that cause the children's learning differences. These lead to their difficulties in adapting to many of the usual ways of teaching. This understanding needs to underpin any assessment of the child's 'ability to do' and prompts the changes in teaching approaches that are necessary if the right kind of support is to be given. This sounds relatively straightforward but the different blends of difficulties that children have, make adjusting teaching input to suit each child a complex undertaking. Teachers will be experts in their field, i.e. in the subject and the children, but children with specific learning difficulties such as dyspraxia will find learning by a 'do this and then that' mode of delivery problematic. They need support with the underlying competencies that so many children and teachers take for granted.

So what are these competencies and how can they be nurtured? They are:

- attending
- concentrating and remembering
- planning and organising.

When asked, most teachers would say that the first two competencies, i.e. 'attending and concentrating' were key indicators of potential success in the classroom. 'Time on task' or how well the children focus, features in many assessments. Teachers tend to see concentration as a measure of a positive attitude, of interest in the topic and potential success. But many young people, particularly those with the attention disorders (ADD and ADHD), but also those with dyslexia and dyspraxia and some on the autistic spectrum, do not pay attention or concentrate spontaneously; they have to be shown how. So helping the children know how to attend and concentrate has to be a vital part of teaching rather than a taken for granted skill. Of course many children without additional support needs will choose not to pay attention if they are not interested or tired or unwell. But this is their choice; they do not have a neurobiological difference such as a poor supply of the neurotransmitter dopamine that is present in ADD/ADHD and possibly in other conditions. This makes staying on task really difficult.

The ability to pay attention and keep on task depends on the children's ability to cut out the distractors in the environment that prevent focusing. Unfortunately auditory and visual distractors influence those with dyspraxia to the extent that they continuously hamper listening to the teacher and seeing what is being displayed. So what can be done? What resources can complement explanations of 'how to pay attention'. Setting up a quiet station to eliminate distractors, e.g. a triangular screen over a writing desk provides a 'private station' and if earphones can be made available to children who are noise hypersensitive, they can have the quiet they need to get on with their work.

Example

Oliver, ten years old

'I always worried about the noise in the classroom and other people moving around all the time really upset me. I found getting any work completed really impossible and I usually had to take it home. Then mum got upset so I didn't tell her and when I got back to school I got another telling off and fell behind with my work although it was easy really. My teacher told me that I wasn't trying, but I was, I really was. I was put in the bottom group, but the children there rustled even more and I just couldn't hear her when she was teaching the whole class.

Eventually my dyspraxia was diagnosed and that was a huge relief. People began to treat me properly and I was much happier. A lady came to the class with my station and some earphones and my life changed. School was much better. When my teacher found out about dyspraxia, she let me use my station whenever I liked and I was able to do much more work without getting a sore head. When she comes by my desk now, she'll say, "Go and run around the hall three times Oliver and then come back and really concentrate for ten minutes." I have a big egg timer so I know that when the sand runs through I put my work in the finished tray. It's usually correct now. I'm also on a listening therapy course and that is helping me to tolerate more noise so I'll not need my station for ever, but just knowing it's there is great.'

Oliver's desk was also moved nearer the teacher and she tried to reduce whole class teaching and do more individual and group work. Oliver's diagnosis had allowed a classroom assistant to be present for part of the day and 'that was a huge help in preparing resources and keeping an eye open for Oliver and others like him who require extra support'.

Helen, Oliver's teacher

'Quite honestly, before his diagnosis, Oliver was a nightmare to have in class. He was always out of his seat, usually complaining of a headache or a sore tummy and he rarely finished his work. I knew he was a bright lad but concentration was nil except for his artwork. He loved that and he could draw amazingly well. He could sit still then. But I had to tell him there were other things to be learned. He didn't do his homework either and wouldn't explain why. Now I realise what was wrong, I feel dreadful but if he had only explained then I could have acted sooner.

Oliver is quite new in this school and at ten his difficulties have been becoming more obvious. After the health visitor observed him, we asked for a referral to a psychologist and we were told he had dyspraxia and was hypersensitive to noise and movement around him. So we set up private stations for three boys who are easily distracted and they have all improved. It's not miraculous, but it's better – at least I know exactly where they should be and they get more work done!

I also decided to change the class timetable so that small groups worked on an integrated day theme. This took a lot of organisation initially but it's made a huge difference to the children with learning differences. They can choose the order of their tasks in the afternoon and they know that they have to be especially attentive when I do teaching with their group. Oliver told me he "saved up all his still time for then", in other words he was making a planned effort to be in control. As his group know that this "control" will be needed immediately after morning break and again after lunch, they can have a good run around in the playground to get rid of surplus energy and come in ready to settle.

Each group in the class now has a daily plan and they can mark off a task when it is completed. This was a system we devised for a child on the autistic spectrum but it is really helpful for many others, in fact I think they all prefer it. Actually this system lets the children plan their day more than before and that's helping those with difficulties develop the planning and organising skills they need.'

Helen raised other important points. The boys 'were out of their seats too much'. It is salutary to recognise that a poor sense of balance could be causing this, because sitting and standing still are the most challenging feats for children who have vestibular sense difficulties. So Helen alerted the physical education teacher and she stressed balance activities in her lessons. She also began a daily motor group so there are more opportunities for children like Oliver to practise and gain confidence on the apparatus.

Observing Oliver writing, Helen noticed that he slouched over his desk. She had thought this was a sign of boredom or laziness but now she recognised that poor muscle tone in his back was making it difficult for him to keep upright. Now aware of his poor muscle tone, she brought him a slightly lower desk and chair so that his feet could rest firmly on the floor. Then he could push up from a strong base. The physiotherapist also gave him special strengthening exercises and advised him to take up swimming. He did this and he loved it. She also gave him a sloping board for his reading and writing so that he didn't have to lean so far forward over his table. Both professionals claimed, 'It's been a long haul but he is thriving now and that's what matters'. They also wondered how they could make this provision for all their children with learning differences? They agreed, 'It's a mammoth task!'

Summary of what can be done

- Provide a triangular station to cut out environmental distractors.
- Check the height of the desk and chair so that the children can be balanced by having their feet supported.
- Organise more one-to-one or small group input rather than whole-class teaching.
- Have a chill-out space where children can go to calm down. Many will feel their anxieties boiling up and know when they have to be excused. Let them choose the time.
- Intersperse activity with short concentrated inputs so that long spells of concentration are broken.

- Recognise and praise 'paying attention' as well as success in oral or written work.
- Let the children know when important spells of concentration are needed so that they can plan ahead!

For most children maturation helps them overcome distractibility, but in dyspraxia this doesn't seem to happen. The children need specific teaching. Wood (1998:56) explains that 'the ability to keep on task and to ignore distractions is a symptom of the structure of the child's intellect and changes in concentration span are related to intellectual development'. So teaching children how to pay attention and concentrate is a key part of helping them to learn.

Memorising

> Deliberate memorising is a learned skill. It does not emerge full-blown at some point of life but involves a series of interlocking activities that eventually become automatic and effortless. But they take time and effort to acquire (Wood, 1998: 57).

So teachers should also use teaching strategies to aid memorising. What could they be?

Youngsters with dyspraxia usually have poor short-term memories. Martin, a twelve-year-old with dyspraxia was asked at 1 pm if he had had lunch at 12 pm, and his blank look revealed he could not remember. He watched the other children going into class and so knew the lunch break was over, so he said 'yes' but, when asked, he had no idea what he had had to eat. But he had developed strategies, i.e. looking at the other children and copying what they were doing, to try to overcome his memory deficit. But what a strain it was, constantly having to devise strategies. Obviously a poor memory is a huge detriment to learning because to learn new things we depend on being able to recall some earlier experience and compare the new with the old. For children with dyspraxia, this is a hard skill. Again many children do this spontaneously without prompting but for others like Martin, teachers have to help them to learn strategies to aid remembering.

Building links and involving visual and motor skills

An interesting activity is to show five- or six-year-old children 20 unrelated pictures or objects and ask them 'How many pictures do you think you will you be able to remember in 10 minutes time?' Very young children are likely to overestimate their recall and be amazed when the practical trial doesn't meet their expectations! However, older ones will be more realistic and as they look at the pictures and they will possibly use a learned strategy, i.e. they will group pictures that have links, e.g. animals or household or fashion items. If they have been taught mind mapping, they may use associations, e.g. they may build a mental picture of a holiday and think of items that they would pack or things they might buy to bring home. So older children, unsurprisingly perhaps, recall more than the younger ones do. However when the young children were allowed to point to the pictures or rearrange them, i.e. when they were encouraged to back up their memory with other sensory input, their scores improved. This is a useful strategy to help children remember and can be useful in supporting children at any age. This would be a technique to try with children with dyspraxia because they would immediately see the success of using such a strategy i.e. using concrete artifacts instead of abstract permutations. They would also recognise that there were ways to overcome poor memories!

Rehearsal and planning

There are many times when rehearsal is a useful strategy. When we have to remember phone numbers as one example, we tend to repeat these until we find a paper and pen to record them. So if children with dyspraxia could be alerted to this technique and be given reminders and opportunities to practise it, then remembering could be eased. One activity could be compiling a shopping list, attempting to repeat the items and then visualising where these things were in the store, e.g. if they knew the fruit was stored by the front door, they could plan to collect it first and put the number one beside the item on their list. If they could draw a rough map of the store layout, they could then add the numbers and make an illustrated list. This longer spell devising strategies could help both memorising and planning ahead. The use of rehearsal might seem to be obvious but children with dyspraxia might not remember to adopt this strategy. They need to be shown how to use it. Even then they might not do so spontaneously but have to make a conscious effort. Many examples when the strategy could be used need to be shared so that they can be encouraged by the number of available possibilities.

Having experienced success, children can see the value of rehearsal and they can apply this to taking notes in class and going over them as soon as possible after the lesson. The timing is important, for a short time between the initial activity and the rehearsal can mean most success. This was discovered when groups of students were asked to recall points of a lesson, shortly after the event, two days and ten days after the teaching. The delay produced marked deterioration in remembering, so immediacy and consistent prompting is needed to aid recall. So perhaps teachers could reduce the number of activities for children with learning difficulties and allow time for reinforcement immediately after teaching input. Children could do this in small groups for teaching each other is a sure way to drive the message home.

Rote learning as an aide-memoire

One much debated strategy is to teach times tables or jingles to help recall of numbers, stories and tales. Rote learning has been called surface learning because it does not involve understanding the deeper meaning of what is being learned. This can be seen when the jingle is remembered long after the learning it was to ease! Many adults remember jingles or times tables but not what they stood for! One early years maths intervention programme asks children to memorise numbers up to 100 in a rhythmical, jingle kind of way. Certainly the children are enthusiastic and appear pleased by their success. The instigators of this approach claim that the 'understanding' of what the numbers mean will come later and more easily if sequences of numbers can be readily recalled. It will be interesting to see if this method of promoting technical mastery then understanding, rather than the two together, works. Could this help young people with dyspraxia who had short-term memory problems? Promoting the memory then the meaning could simplify the task?

Critics of rote learning explain that although instant recall of facts may be possible the lack of any contextualisation means that there is no real understanding and little possibility of transfer of learning from one situation to another.

The debate about the place of rote learning is not new. Those who follow Piaget's ideology would claim that rote learning leads to empty procedural knowledge, and that children should not be exposed to learning beyond their stage of understanding. However, Vygotsky and Bruner see rote learning as 'the raw material of learning and development'. They see rote learning as a social activity and a form of developing expertise.

Example

Sarah and her daughter

One mum, Sarah, told me that she had bought a tape of times tables with music. This had lots of repetition of tables at different speeds and whenever she was in the car with her daughter who was dyspraxic, she played the tape. Sometimes they repeated the jingles together, other times the tape just played with her little girl seemingly paying little heed. But the regularity and the repetition paid off, at least at the level of instant recall, and the little girl was so pleased to be able to answer quickly and correctly in class. Sarah explained, 'We had to keep at it and at it. Some days she seemed to have forgotten lots of answers she knew before. It wasn't easy and sometimes it was difficult for both of us not to show our frustration. However we devised a "whoops" game and when answers didn't come readily we'd say "Whoops!" This sounds strange, but it took the pressure off and made us smile. I knew if I got cross, that would be the end of the practising, so "whoops" was a strategy to keep the routine going.'

Advance organisers

Children with dyspraxia often have difficulty remembering what went before, e.g. the content of previous lessons, and so it is very useful to have 'advance organisers' or recaps such as giving youngsters time to read previously corrected notes at the start of any new input. These could also be pictures or tapes or videos to prod the memories of children with difficulties before the new lesson begins. Thus the children's recall is supported and they can use that previous knowledge as a building block for the new learning that is about to happen.

So what is the memory and what is happening in our brains when we remember things?

Carter (2000: 261) explains that the memory is 'many things'. It allows you to swim or ride a bike when it's a long time since you tried; it's the thing that allows you to recognise friends and remember all about them; it causes you to be afraid in situations where unhappy events took place and at night it conjures up fragments of previous experiences and puts them together, often illogically as dreams. It lets taxi drivers find destinations in intricate streets without resource to maps; it gives old people pleasure or stress as they recall clearly what happened years ago but no longer remember what went on yesterday. It provides a base for new learning. What is happening in the brain to ensure these memories exist?

Memories are made in individual cells in an associated group. When one neuron in the group fires, they all fire, creating a specific pattern. A group of neurons firing together in the auditory area might recall the sound of a particular piece of music. Another group might react to the taste of a food or drink and remind the person of another time when these tastes were experienced. The important thing is that the pattern remains after the stimulus, in this second case after the food or drink is finished. The longevity of the memories depends on their repetition because if stimuli are repeated the same groups of cells fire and the pattern becomes encoded firming up their association with a meaningful place or event. When neurons fire they set off an electrical charge that stimulates their neighbours and a chemical change takes place that leaves the partner cell more vulnerable to a repeat firing. In this way a memory is formed. There are four different kinds of memory depending on the function that is to be carried out.

These are:

1   procedural memory: this is the memory that enables us to ride a bike, drive a car or make a cake without up-to-date instruction. We don't forget the skills that have been learned with joy and probably practised regularly at the start.
2   fear memory: phobias and negative emotions are stored in the amygdala, part of the limbic system and they can cause depression.
3   episodic memory: personal memories are interpreted by the hippocampus and stored in the cortex. Personal memories are more easily recalled because of the associations they have with people who appear regularly or who have strong emotional bonds.
4   semantic memory: this is the memory that records facts. These are interpreted in the cortical areas and stored in the temporal lobe.

Not all thoughts are stored as memories. As one thought passes, another takes its place. Yet when these thoughts are linked with emotions or important personal events they become meaningful; they are stored in the long-term memory and can be recalled many years after the incident that stimulated them. So teachers have to try to help children to contextualise their thinking, i.e. to link new ideas to something meaningful and relevant in their personal experience so that important items pass into the long-term memory store.

Organisation and planning

Young people who have dyspraxia definitely need to be shown how to organise and plan their work, for inability to do so can mean that perfectly intelligent people cannot get things ready in time. The organisation defeats their imagination.

Example

Gordon

'All my life I have wanted to be a teacher. I had a relatively mild form of dyspraxia so I had to work extra hard to get the grades I needed. I really looked forward to being involved with young children because I enjoyed school myself. But when placement in school came around I just couldn't cope. I had planned lessons according to the advice given in the university but putting the ideas into action in the classroom was impossible. I had to think of where the different children would be at any time in the day and know what they were all doing. At the same time I had to get the teaching resources ready, not just for one lesson but the next one too. The subject knowledge was OK but the organisation defeated me. I was distraught.'

Marie

At a much earlier stage, seven-year-old Marie found organising herself very difficult too. 'When I was small, mum did most things for me including checking what I needed for school, so I had only to pick up my bag in the morning. I managed fine. But then at Brownies I had the chance to go to camp and mum thought I should try to get things ready myself. The problem was I couldn't picture what I'd need. I was stumped. So we drew out a timetable. Mum said "Imagine one part of the day at a time" but it was too difficult so I said I had a sore tummy and didn't go.'

In class children with dyspraxia need a great deal of support to overcome their planning difficulties. There is a subtle but important distinction between helping children complete the end product, be it a painting, a model or a puzzle, and helping them with the process – the organisation of materials and stage-by-stage completion of the task. Asking 'Tell me what you want to do' is the key to knowing whether planning is a problem. The follow-on, 'Well, what will you do first?', tells whether organisation is difficult. Teachers need to distinguish between planning and organisational difficulties and conceptual/understanding difficulties if their support is to be appropriate. In story writing, for example, children will be frustrated to be given 'more words' to make their story more imaginative, if sequencing is the real problem. In free play activities, or with older children compiling projects, adults trying to be helpful often suggest imaginative ideas, e.g. 'Why don't you do …?' The result is that inadvertently the ownership of the play or the project transfers to the adult. The young people lose control of the development and they then have to await further instruction from the adult because they didn't know her intention. And of course most children comply with the adults' ideas, believing that these experts know best. But when the children already have the ideas of how to develop their play or their project, what they are likely to need are ideas about structuring the development, perhaps subdividing the whole into manageable chunks and compiling a timetable of events or it might be simply knowing how to organise the resources to make their plan happen. There is a conceptual difference in supporting planning and organising and providing the ideas, i.e. adopting a top-down model of instruction.

Problem-solving strategies: transfer of learning

Another 'special skill' is building a range of problem-solving strategies so that when a problem is encountered, children can select the most appropriate and effective way of solving it. The process of making children aware of the different strategies they use is called metacognition. This sounds very helpful – if children are made aware of what they do and what they could do, surely they will use the more successful way? The snag is that alerting the children to a successful problem-solving strategy is a far cry from getting them to recall it and select it when a similar problem arises. This is why transfer of learning from one situation to another doesn't readily occur, even although it is difficult to understand why not.

It is also worth remembering that different children learn best in different ways. Many listening activities will suit some children and defeat those who learn best by seeing. Other children like to have 'hands-on' experiences and interactive activities help them retain the key learning points. Many dyspraxic children with tactile hypersensitivity, however, will not be happy to have 'feely bag' activities because of the sensitivity in their hands. Some will simply refuse to take part.

As teachers, we can be guilty of preparing learning materials to suit our own preferred way of learning because this is what comes naturally. To help dyspraxic children, however, we must identify their preferred way and know how to support them in the process of learning. This involves planning, organising and remembering perhaps even more than the subject matter itself. Teachers have to decentre to understand the thought processes and difficulties of children with learning differences. This is very difficult and time consuming but the reward comes when the children's faces light up and they begin to enjoy learning for its own sake.

Chapter 5

Social development and making friends

The first relationships children have are with their parents, and clinics and reading materials all emphasise the importance of early bonding. Ainsworth (1972) identified this term, defining it as 'the strong and long lasting affectional tie formed between baby and parents'. She also held that if bonding did not happen, then later relationships could be affected. Immediately parents who considered that they had not been able to create this bond felt cheated or guilty or inadequate. Now the timing of bonding has been widened. It is now thought to depend on 'the pattern of interlocking behaviours which develop over the first weeks and months' (Bee, 2004). 'Having time' is a comfort for those who have fretful infants or premature babies which need intensive care and can't be at home in the early weeks or for those that suffer the 'baby blues'. Understandably mums who are disappointed that their baby has a disability could be in this group.

Often poor muscle tone makes babies who are later found to have dyspraxia very floppy. Mums often say, 'I knew from the first moment there was something wrong', but their concerns are often brushed aside as being caused by over-anxiety. Some of these babies are not easy to rear. Poor muscle tone in the mouth makes sucking difficult and if breastfed babies 'have to work much harder' (Goddard, 2008) this may be impossible. Prolonged sucking with no success may cause them to be irritable, especially if they sense that their parents are tense, and some hardly need any sleep. 'She only ever slept for three hours at a time', explained one distraught mum. 'I'd spend hours persuading her to feed then she seemed to be awake again before I had everything tidied up. It was frantic!' This can put a strain on bonding especially if the parents think they must be doing something wrong or if they are disappointed or exhausted by the way their baby behaves. Another difficulty in forming relationships comes if the child does not or cannot hold eye contact and smile. These are particularly rewarding episodes for tired parents, but sadly many children with dyspraxia avoid eye contact, so this way into bonding is lost. This communication, this mutuality appears to underlie much of the security and pleasure that parent and child derive from each other. Poor muscle tone also means that children will show delay in achieving their motor milestones. This causes anxiety too although parents can be assured that their children will go through the same stages as others, but more slowly. These delays can stress parents but sound relationships can still be built, perhaps best when expectations become realistic, when outside pressures are ignored and when everyone begins to relax and realise that learning to be a parent takes time and practice. It is important to persevere. Schaffer (1989) urges parents to do all they can to build a positive early relationship with their child, for 'the establishment of the child's primary social relationships is generally considered to constitute the foundation on which all psychosocial behaviour is based'.

How does this psychosocial behaviour develop? Fagot and Pears (1996) claim that children who have secure attachments at home are 'more likely to be altruistic or create more reciprocal friendships'. But what if this doesn't happen? What if the child comes home from school and repeatedly says he has no friends?

One of the saddest things is to hear children say, 'No one will let me play', and this can worry parents more than any academic difficulties. The parents of dyspraxic children know their children are bright and they so want them to be happy at school and they feel that that comes from having friends. A tremendous feeling of helplessness comes with the realisation that many, if not most children with dyspraxia are destined to be loners or worse, the victim of bullies who pick on anyone they see as being different. Very often dyspraxic children, because of their impulsivity and having to be supervised all the time, are more sheltered at home than others in their peer group. They therefore face a bigger challenge when they come to school. If their planning skills are poor, they may have more difficulty visualising what the day holds and they will be tentative and possibly reluctant to join in. This can make them vulnerable and when they can't tie laces or play football or ride a bike either, all 'public' differences, then they tend to be left out. Jake found this. He explained, 'When we go to the gym, no one will take me for a partner. If it's games, I play with the teacher usually or I have to go into a three and they sometimes look angry. Why am I always the last to be picked?' Naturally, the children feel and look sad and resentful and this can add to their isolation. Social skills play a part too, for when table manners become important and finger food no longer suffices as party fare, then the children who can't use a knife and fork or who spill and break things are left out and of course the children don't understand why: 'There's another party and I'm not invited again mum, why not?'

When do these difficulties begin? Isolation may not be apparent at nursery, for at this stage children are egocentric, i.e. they are almost completely tied up in their own concerns. They play near one another rather than with one another in any real or sustained way. At this stage they have the language to make interactions happen, but not yet the empathy or sympathy to sustain them. They work in groups, perhaps baking cakes, but they are usually checking that they get their allotted turns rather than being worried about how anyone else is faring. Development however means change, and soon it is important to the children that they are welcomed as part of a group and a little later that they have a best friend.

The importance of being the same

Even in the first years at school, and parents say 'earlier and earlier', children want to be the same, hence the pleas for the same clothes and trainers, the same haircuts and computer games. They instinctively feel that this will help them to be one of the gang, a position that prevents them being 'left out'. Few children have the courage to go out of their way to include a child who is ignored or rejected by the popular ones, even though some who have a well-developed sense of altruism know that they should.

Children tend to choose friends from those who are like them; they have a strong sense of 'us and them' and will jealously guard against intrusion. Even in the younger age groups many children have strong stereotypes of those who are 'not like me'. This is why children from ethnic minority groups gravitate to their own kind at seven or so (Aboud and Doyle, 2005). This is quite natural it seems, for the children are establishing the mores of their own culture.

This solidarity is more evident with boys' groups especially when they are quite newly formed. This 'wanting to be part of a group' can even cause clever children to deliberately underachieve in school, as 'being different' means being left out. It is not difficult to see where parents' goals and children's ways diverge. Choosing friends at an early age can depend on children's rather superficial judgments that cover concrete rather than abstract factors. Some fascinating research by Edinburgh teaching students asked children of different ages to describe their best friend.

Example

Craig

Six-year-old Craig volunteered to talk about Sam, his 'special friend':
'He's a big, big fellow – huge really, with big feet and he sometimes falls over and bangs into me. He has fair hair and usually is kind, but not always for we fall out. He has a rabbit and a dog and I wish I had one too. Sam stays in quite a wee house with a green door at the front.'

As you can see his comments were mainly about appearances – surface qualities rather than enduring factors. Eleven-year-old Gemma's account of her friend Lynn, was quite different.

Example

Gemma

'I'll tell you about Lynn. She's my very best friend because she's always smiling. She gets us all organised. She's the captain of our netball team and she's really dependable at turning up and giving her best shot. The good thing is that if we lose she doesn't blame one person because we are a team. That helps if the shooters have a bad day. She's not very clever but she copes and doesn't mind too much. She giggles a lot and keeps us all cheery.'

Gemma was much more concerned with attitudes and capabilities, i.e. deeper and more long-lasting attributes than those which concerned Craig, and these reports were typical of the children's comments at each age.

This should offer comfort to parents of dyspraxic children – friendship patterns may change once the children's deeper qualities become part of the equation. This will happen more readily if the children in the class have no established pecking order that has endured for some time, but nonetheless friendship patterns do change as the children mature. Perhaps explaining the nature of dyspraxia to the other children could encourage empathy and dispel any strange notions, e.g. that they might catch this illness if they take hands or play together.

Having the same interests

When children move beyond the boundaries of their family to find friends, the peer group becomes very important. At age six or seven, cooperative play develops with children playing together for some sustained time. At this age the activity the children prefer to do is very important. Bee (2004) tells us that shared interests continue to form the major basis of young children's relationships. And so, one way for adults to try helping children who don't get to play, is to find the kind of thing they really enjoy doing and then plan how this could be introduced into the curriculum, or find ways in which the child might be able to join others who also like that kind of activity at recreation or home times.

This sounds straightforward, but of course the child who has caused all this concern may not want to join the children who are engrossed in his kind of activity. He may know exactly who he wants to join and be willing to risk rejection rather than settling for another group of children. Liam did this. Although his teacher knew he was very interested in animals – and asked him to bring in his favourite book to share with a group of children who enjoyed animals too – this didn't work because Liam still wanted to be a part of the dominant group in the class, i.e. the group he saw as being made up of the popular children. This activity-based strategy very often does help however, and the planning involves:

1   finding the child's interests and preparing a new initiative based on that (this is so that the child doesn't have the difficulty of breaking into an already established game);
2   setting up the appropriate resources, hoping that interested children will come to play; or, if that fails
3   inviting a group of like-minded children to join in.

But why should some children's company be sought and others shunned?

The characteristics of popular and rejected children

Some of the qualities that cause children to be left out are beyond their control, which seems most unfair. Physically larger, but slim, better looking children, especially if they have sunny temperaments, tend to be the most popular. Perhaps being popular allows them to smile more? It is difficult certainly for rejected children to smile; they are understandably sulky or aggressive or withdrawn – all factors which cause the rejection to be sustained. This is often the fate of obese children, as is name calling. These children are rejected and ridiculed and are often driven to seek comfort in eating more. Sadly, they sometimes have other negative qualities attributed to them as well – laziness and stupidity (Bryne 2003) even when there is no evidence to bear this out. Seeing this happen, 'fear of being fat' can cause even children of eight or nine to diet, even to have anorexia.

Popular children are 'non-aggressive; they explain things; they take their playmates' views into consideration; they are able to regulate their expression of strong emotions' (Pettit *et al.* 1996). In other words they can read other people's reactions and adjust their own behaviour accordingly; they have a well-developed emotional intelligence and are consistently positive. On the other hand, rejected children are often disruptive; they spoil games by being over loud and boisterous or, in an attempt to show power, they themselves reject children who offer to play. Youngsters who have dyspraxia sometimes see aggression as the way to solve their difficulties. If they are involved in even a slight accident, they may interpret any bump as 'meant', i.e. as a deliberate act against them, and they retaliate in a hostile way in return. This just makes everything worse.

While children do offer support to their friends and develop empathy and altruism as they mature, they also tease, argue and fight, in other words they use aggressive behaviours. Some children will do this much more with their siblings at home – indeed parents with several youngsters sometimes compare their home territory to a war zone! Of course, only children don't have this opportunity to try out different strategies for getting their own way and may save their aggression for school, or they may retreat from the fray, unsure as to the consequences of becoming involved; alternatively, they may be naturally placid children. But patterns of aggression do change and there are important differences in the ways in which boys and girls vent their feelings.

Patterns of aggression

In the early years children are likely to use physical violence and they will hit out if their wishes are thwarted. But as their verbal skills improve, this method of retaliation diminishes and they use taunts or name calling instead. Boys in junior school relish competition/dominance/physical aggression more than girls, a finding which endorses gender stereotyping. They tend to gather in larger groups and move further from home. None of these attributes is likely to help children with dyspraxia make friends. When Maccoby (1990) carried out her study of children making friends, she found that the patterns of interaction used by the two sexes were qualitatively different. Whereas girls used explanations and asked, 'Can I have a turn?' boys grabbed what they wanted, exclaiming, 'Give me that!' This may well explain why shy or introverted boys prefer to play with girls, for they feel unable to cope with aggressive behaviour.

Another pattern that is not popular is coercive behaviour, where children use emotional blackmail to gain what they want. Other children recognise this, and while they may applaud it in a popular child who uses it infrequently to gain an advantage for the group, they deride it in a less popular child who uses it to gain a personal advantage. If these children have been 'successful' at home, through building a coercive attachment pattern with their parents who perhaps want to compensate the child for not having friends at school, then the children will try this behaviour at school and be confused and distressed when it does not work. The trouble is that rejected children often find that the only group that welcomes them is made up of other rejected children, and the role model *they* provide may not be helpful at all.

And so children can inadvertently build barriers to friendship, and the sadness is that not getting to play at age four often means the same at eight and ten. But this need not persist. Children can change their ways once they are able to understand that others have needs; once they are aware of the perspectives of others and how their own behaviour impacts on their chance of becoming an accepted member of the group. Some children, unhappily, find great difficulty in making this change. This is an important finding to confirm the notion of giving children labels to explain their difficulties.

Understanding other people's perceptions: the development of a theory of mind

At around two years of age, children begin to understand that other people have intentions and that their behaviour will mirror these, e.g. if a child looks longingly at a cake, the likelihood is that he will try to get it. By three this kind of understanding deepens – the children begin to develop theories: 'If that person believes this, he is likely to do this, or perhaps that'. They also start to realise that someone may still want something, even though he can't have it. The understanding however has not deepened to the extent that they realise that other people may act on beliefs that are incorrect.

At age four or five, there are still aspects of other people's thinking to be grasped. The four-year-old understands 'I know that you know', but does not appreciate that this process is reciprocal. Such understanding develops for most children around ages five to seven. This is a critical stage in the development of genuine reciprocal friendship. If two children, at different levels of development and therefore understanding, try to make friends, it is not difficult to see how misunderstandings, which are developmental rather than intentional, arise. Most preschool children can accurately read the facial expressions for 'happy' or 'sad' but hardly any can deal with 'proud' or 'guilty'. This is complex enough for children without specific difficulties. How much harder it is for those who have real problems in this perceptual area, e.g. for children on the autistic spectrum. Some children with dyspraxia have this difficulty too.

One piece of advice given to support these children is to immerse them in social encounters so that they have plenty of opportunity to see different modes of interaction although these need to be explained, e.g. 'Did you notice that when Brook wanted to join in, she waited till the group was busy and then slipped into the group? She didn't ask or shout, she just watched for an appropriate moment and joined in. Let's watch this other group and choose a moment when you could do that'.

Children without siblings and self-sufficient children who are content to play alone or in a very small group are more likely to have difficulty with interpretation of emotions and subsequent actions, than children who have a wider social group (Lewis, 2005). The dilemma of artificially engineering sympathetic encounters against knowing that this is not reality is a difficult one to resolve. Perhaps the answer is to take one stage at a time and above all to keep the interactions calm and stress free.

Joining a self-help group

One dad, Graeme, joined a self-help group because he anticipated that having children with learning differences/difficulties together would be a good way for them to make friends, because 'they'd all have the same kinds of social problems'. He thought there would be a shared understanding that would promote friendships. When he took his eleven-year-old son, Kerr, to the group however, the lad retreated and just sat in a corner, overwhelmed by the size of the company and the noise. Graeme decided to persevere and after about six increasingly successful sessions his son volunteered to lead some of the craft activities. How had this happened? Graeme explained, 'One of the older children who was managing to overcome some of his own difficulties encouraged him and this was marvellous. I could have hugged that child. He comes regularly to play at our house now and although they still tend to play at different things, Kerr likes his stamp album while Gary prefers computer games, but at least there are two of them together in the room and Kerr can tell everyone at school about "his friend". I don't think anyone who has not experienced it can understand the horror of the day when your child tells you he doesn't have any friends.'

And so, although the boys were not playing together in any cooperating sense, they tolerated each other and respected what the other was trying to do. The important thing was that they were able to talk about 'my friend'. Both sets of parents reported the 'huge relief' that this brought. One dad explained, 'My whole day is a lot brighter. A dark cloud has lifted. I don't worry nearly so much now'. But establishing the friendship had taken much time and effort. It was not just a case of putting children together.

Another mum fell foul of the same scheme. Her son Paul ran out from the group shouting, 'I'm not like them. Why would I want to play with them?' So children with difficulties themselves can be just as intolerant as others. It is so difficult to get it right!

Differences in children that make it difficult for them to play

Children with dyspraxia very often find it impossible to play games that others have planned. They have enough difficulty in planning what they themselves wish to do in a 'this then that' sequence of events. Given that this is problematic, they are even less likely to be able to interpret someone else's plans and appreciate the emotions that disrupting them could engender. Many games have unwritten rules; children just seem to absorb them from experience. For those who have not got this facility, sustaining friendships can be very difficult.

Youngsters who can't do the movement skills which other children value, e.g. play football or ride a bike, tend to get left out when their more physically able friends go off or join teams. If they feel they have broken into a group and then they are left out again, this may well cause anxiety, even depression. A good idea is to fund coaching of basic movement patterns or even better, request/insist that the school provides extra coaching.

Children with ADHD (attention deficit hyperactivity disorder) have similar difficulties even though the cause is different. These children are extremely restless. This prevents concentration for themselves and causes disruption and annoyance to others. They have a deficit in the ability to inhibit behaviour; they must react to any stimulus. Their problem is much more severe than that of the 'normally' restless child who is often urged to sit still. When other children get angry at being disturbed, these children can't alter their behaviour to comply and resentment builds up. Sometimes naughty children will provoke them as a way of setting up a distraction in the class. Their high level of impulsivity and lack of ability to concentrate also means that they cannot participate in any sustained game. Children with dyspraxia can have overlapping ADHD and may find the same reaction from children in their class.

It is not surprising to find that many children who can't make friends display excessive aggressiveness. Unfortunately, this compounds their difficulty. This combination may well lead to them bullying or being bullied. Delinquency is sometimes the resort of children who are miserable and withdrawn. They 'get back' at society by showing disdain for its rules. This is one way of making sense of their existence.

On a much less sombre note, some dyspraxic children take the content of conversations too literally; they don't see the joke or appreciate the innuendo. One boy explained, 'I see them all laugh, so I go "Ha ha" too, but I really don't know why!' Teasing can be especially hurtful for these children, who, unable to understand laughing with others, certainly won't be able to laugh at themselves. They also have difficulty realising that some comments are not meant to be taken literally, but shrugged off, not to be taken to heart. If the offending child is then taken to task, resentment builds up. This is the kind of situation that leads to children being avoided and acts against children being able to make friends. How do adults begin to explain this to children?

Children with any kind of learning difficulty often have related social problems that make matters worse. The trouble is that because they are individuals with their own personality factors and because they are brought up in different environments with different value systems and cultural practices, there is not one recipe which will be guaranteed to help them all.

Mixed-age classrooms

McClelland and Kinsey (1996) offer one solution. They found that if children experiencing difficulties in making friends could be incorporated into classes with younger children, the problem was often eased. These younger children did not make the same social demands. Moreover, they respected the older ones simply because of their age, and there was a chance for a new, positive start. Parents of dyspraxic youngsters often find that their children prefer the company of younger ones. A small school with several age groups together could well help.

Parenting styles

The family plays a vital role in the social development of their children. Knowing this, parents of young people with dyspraxia often wonder if they have done something wrong. 'Did I not pay enough attention, or give too much?' is a commonly asked question. The answer is that concerned parents are not to blame for usually they have done all they can in terms of understanding the condition and trying to find sources of help. There is no universal recipe, which will guarantee success in bringing up any child, and this may be because different individual children interacting with their own parents present a unique set of characteristics. Families that have positive, helpful children however would usually claim to have provided an environment that shows:

- warmth or nurturance
- appropriately high expectations
- honest interactions
- consistent standards and rules.

This consistency is vitally important to youngsters with dyspraxia because of their difficulty in understanding and adapting to change. Established routines allow them to carry out everyday tasks competently and earn praise. For this reason, some prefer to stay indoors at playtime especially when they have the legitimate excuse of helping the teacher. This is a kindly way to relieve some of the pressure of the day, because these children often feel happier indoors. This also saves the miseries of donning outdoor wear then changing back within a short time and finding once more that they don't get to play.

But of course not all children develop in the same way and this is as true for children with dyspraxia as any other. Some are anxious to take every learning opportunity while others are reluctant and shy. The effects from the children's environment are complex and pervasive. Schools must try to understand all the implications of having dyspraxia and compensate for any disadvantages so that the children have the best possible chance to realise their potential. This is not an easy thing to do.

Being bullied

Having few friends is bad enough but no child should have to tolerate being bullied, yet this often happens whenever a vulnerable child is seen as being different. Perhaps the dyspraxic youngsters' inability to share jokes because they take conversations too literally or their sometimes erratic or inappropriate behaviour sets them apart and they make easy targets. By the middle years of childhood, children are old enough to realise the implications of their behaviour on others and vindictive children can spark off scenes when they know other children will be blamed. Even when this is recognised and the real perpetrators are named, some will say they are sorry while others show no remorse at all. Some children will remain impassive even in the face of the other children's distress and some even retaliate by being even more aggressive later. Observations like this cause us to ask if such aggressive children are hostile all of the time or if their attitude is context specific? If teachers can find out what is causing the anger and correct it, will all be well? Murray and Keane (1998) found that although many children could be both sunny and hostile, there were sadistic bullies who responded to their siblings' distress with glee. A chilling thought.

From this research, we can gather that some children learn how to inflict hurt but never learn to sympathise. Sometimes explanations of bad behaviour, e.g. 'you mustn't hit because it is really painful', can even stimulate further aggression towards the damaged child. And so no one can expect all children to develop altruism, or even with explanation, develop caring and sympathetic ways. Sadly, bullies can attract other children who decide to join them simply to stop themselves becoming a target. There are many policies on bullying now. Where can help be found?

Where to get help

The Dyspraxia Foundation in 'Seeing your way through' (1998) offers practical advice to children who have been bullied and to their parents. This is because inappropriate and possibly emotional intervention can make things worse, yet how can parents stand by and do nothing? The children are advised to write down or have someone else scribe the events that occurred. This is so that they can recount them to someone they trust without getting flustered and so losing the sequence of what occurred. When the bullying is actually taking place, they are advised to keep calm and only repeat a statement which they have practised beforehand, saying for example, 'My name is Helen. I don't want any other name', or 'I want you to leave me alone'. They must not be goaded into retaliating, either verbally or physically. The main advice is to tell someone trustworthy in authority – then these people must take steps. They are legally bound to do so. It may help children to know that 15 per cent of all children are bullied. While this is a sad indictment of our young people, the figures can show the bullied children that they are not alone and very importantly, that they are not to blame.

Many children will try to hide the fact that they are being bullied because 'at school no one has time to listen', and at home, 'Mum'll go up to school and the others will know it's me that's told', or 'You just have to put up with it. My dad says he was bullied too'. The above reasons show why many parents are uneasy, even afraid that going to school will make things worse for their child. But if they do nothing the bullies have won. And if the school does not take steps to help, then action should be taken against them too. Sometimes schools are unaware that bullying is going on and indeed some children can be oversensitive to a single playground remark. But when aggression, likely to be verbal rather than physical in the six to fourteen age range, is happening regularly and if the child is affected through crying or being withdrawn or having pains or wanting to go home, these signs must be investigated. Sometimes bullies are being bullied themselves and are venting their own power over a more fearful child. Very often they are insecure themselves. Whatever the reason, they cannot be allowed to harm other children. Parents should ask to see the school's policy on bullying and then they will be able to identify procedures. This can provide a focus for discussion with the head teacher. All of this takes courage, but if the parents are afraid and hesitate, then they must imagine and take the blame for the effect continued bullying has on their child.

Of course many bullies are too devious to be caught and may accost the vulnerable children once they have left school. If this happens, the school may feel that they cannot take the responsibility for what goes on outside their premises. The only solution is to have the child met and inform the police. The bullied child may not want this, but he has to be kept safe.

Developing empathy

It is apparent then that children differ in the extent to which they can empathise with the feelings of another child and that some simply cannot appreciate another child's distress when they themselves do not feel it. They therefore cannot appreciate the perspective of another person. Different children have different levels of emotional development just as they differ intellectually or in their movement skills. But emotional development is awesome, in that failure to develop it hurts others and eventually the children themselves. Some children of course have aggressive role models and may be copying patterns of behaviour they see at home. If these children can be helped to decentre, i.e. to understand the implications of their actions for others and realise that in the longer term their peers will resent their behaviour, then perhaps they may try to change. This can be attempted through classroom discussions in a personal and social development programme or through role-play in drama, when the suspected bully may take the place of his tormented 'friend'.

The capacity to understand that someone else is happy or sad or proud of some achievement brings with it an appreciation of 'why', i.e. the underlying events that have caused that emotion. If they appreciate someone else's emotion, do they feel it themselves? The answer could be 'yes' or 'no' depending on the type of event as well as the personality of the child. Think of watching a sad film. Children and adults weep when ET goes home or when the Snowman melts. They know it is just a story and yet emotions overtake cold logic. The audience has empathised; they have felt the emotions of the characters in the play. The film makers have portrayed experiences that children can relate to quite easily, and adults can remember with nostalgia – all that is required is a 'temporary suspension of disbelief in the fiction that has been created' (Harris, 1992). Is this what drama in school tries to do? Is the aim to encourage a deeper understanding of other people's feelings and through that their lives? Can children really understand what it is like to be someone else, perhaps a child who has dyspraxia, or is this a charade? Do they need experiences or can they imagine the implications in their heads? If they can't, how are they to learn to empathise with those that are less fortunate than themselves? Is there any real hope of beating the bullies till they do?

Developing prosocial or altruistic behaviour

The development of altruism or prosocial behaviour shows age changes just as all other aspects of development do. Altruism is 'intentional voluntary behaviour intended to benefit another' (Eisenberg, 1992), and usually this is at some cost to oneself.

This was just a practical, 'research' way of checking out the claims about the age-related development of altruism made in the literature. But why should children respond in different ways? Does their society and/or their culture influence their behaviour? Would the overt things the children said they would do, have happened in reality?

Example

A small piece of research illustrates this well. Children of different ages were told a story and then asked separately, 'If you were there, what would you do?'

The story

'You are rollerblading through the park with your friends on the way to a pizza place where you will all have a party. On the way you see a boy/girl who has fallen and is hurt. If you were there, what would you do?'

The researchers found that it was important to offer a boy or a girl as the injured one in the story, as one girl, in a pilot study which only had only included boys, replied, 'I'd do nothing – I hate all boys!' With this adjustment, the replies from children in the subsequent study were fascinating and clearly showed how altruism developed over the junior years.

Children's replies

Alice aged four:
'Well ... well, I'm really wee and if I saw a policeman I'd tell him. But I couldn't wait to help because I'd get lost.'

Alice wasn't really going to help for the very understandable and legitimate reason of 'getting lost', but she was aware that she should do something – tell a policeman!

Jimmy aged six:
'I'd give him my blades to get home. He'd have to write down his address. But then I'd not be able to keep up with my pals – no wait. I'd help him over to the park bench and then a grown-up would see him.'

Jimmy knew he should help. He was able to conceptualise a plan – even though he hadn't thought of how an injured child could use his blades. He already had a street-wise awareness – the boy might steal his blades – and in the end, concern for himself won!

Rob aged nine:
'I'd pick him up and put him on my back and we'd both go to the pizza place because I would have enough money to pay for us both, or I'd phone his home on my mobile and tell his mother where he was ... then I'd catch up on the others.'

Rob had two strategies to help. He obviously preferred the second, but given that he couldn't make contact with the boy's mother, he was prepared not to abandon the child. Altruism is growing.

Rebecca aged eleven:
'I'd first of all check how badly she was hurt and if it was serious I'd get someone to phone for an ambulance. If it was a sprain I'd just wait with her till someone came along or she was able to put her weight on it.'

Asked if she wouldn't mind missing her treat she said, 'Oh no', and she looked quite superior, knowing that she had said the 'right thing'. Then she spoiled it somewhat, by adding, 'I hate pizza anyway!'

Rebecca had a much clearer idea of what society expected and she was prepared to fulfil that role. She had thought about the situation much more than the others, in that she considered different degrees of hurt, and was ready to have someone phone for an ambulance. She was totally confident and in charge of events. Do you think she was envisaging other kinds of spin-offs for herself, perhaps relaying the story later and being applauded or seeing inside the A & E department? Or was she prepared to give up her treat with no thought of gain for herself? This would be the case in real altruism!

Eisenberg (1992) explains that very young children of three or so, will offer a toy or cuddle to another child who has been hurt. They will wrap their arms around and murmur soothing words. These children are just beginning to understand about the emotions of others and are newly able to respond to them. Older children offer more in the way of toys or material comforts but less physical contact. (Rob's picking the child up was a means of transport, not comfort!) Do these gestures mirror practices at home? Perhaps these deliberations and actions reflect the parents' ways of giving reassurance, i.e. with less physical contact as their children mature? There may be a gender difference here – certainly more boys tend to shy way from overt, especially public demonstrations of emotion. The different ways families show emotion must influence the children's behaviour, and of course this may be the mode of the specific cultural group as well. And so there are many influences and it is not easy to understand where they have come from or interpret exactly what they mean.

Children with dyspraxia may not fully appreciate the subtleties that come with emotional development. Parents are therefore urged to:

- Create a warm, loving climate, and say, 'Let's have a happy, quiet time together'. This shows the child that his company is important to you, especially when he is good.
- Explain the best way to respond in different situations.
- Make up stories like the pizza one (see above) and discuss the implications of several hypothetical replies. Don't take it for granted that the child will absorb and copy the family's way of behaving. Explain that, 'It's always best to be helpful because you will feel good too' or 'Jane is sad today because her dog has died. Stay with her quietly. Don't speak about Toby – just be there for her, and she'll know you care'.
- Give lots of praise immediately after the event and say why it has been earned. Not 'Good chap' but 'Good for you tidying your room without being asked. That's a big help'. This is much more likely to reinforce the behaviour and for it to happen again. This is especially important if the praise has to come some time after the event because the short-term memory difficulty can cause children to forget. In that case, 'That's good' loses impact, because the child does not remember how the praise was earned. Provide opportunities for children to do helpful things. In today's climate of rushing everywhere, it can be so much easier and quicker, and possibly cheaper (because of breakages!) just to do the jobs yourself. But obvious jobs left undone can help the child to contribute and let him see that you can be 'forgetful' or a bit slapdash too! A

'buddy atmosphere' can change the power status and make it easier for children who know they are often inept to take part in the daily routine. This also allows them to practise their coping skills.

- Be a generous, helpful role model. Youngsters with dyspraxia find it easier to do as you do rather than what they know you should do! This is because they may well have difficulty fitting the correct actions to different situations.

Interpreting and analysing and responding to emotional behaviour is difficult and upsetting when it goes wrong. How much more difficult is it for children with dyspraxia who lack the facility to interpret others' cues?

Chapter 6

Emotional development

The self-concept

Everyone hopes that their children will be happy and confident and be able to make the most of all the opportunities that come their way. To do this they need to have a positive self-concept. When children have a learning difference, a specific learning difficulty or a disability, their families are naturally very concerned that their children's self-concept will be harmed. What do they mean? Why should this happen? What will the implications be? These are important questions for all those who interact with children, with any kind of difficulty, for they are likely to be the most sensitive and vulnerable, possibly even seeing slights where none was intended. Certainly if people concentrate on children's difficulties without producing appropriate learning materials so that the children can succeed and thus have lots of genuine positive feedback, their opinion of themselves, i.e. their self-esteem will not be high.

What then is the self-concept?

The self-concept is the name given to the picture children build of themselves through their interactions with others. This picture is formed as a result of quite an intricate, ongoing evaluation, sometimes called a tri-dimensional image. This is explained by the words, 'What I think of myself depends on what I think you think of me!'

Cooley (1962) called this 'the looking glass self', a name that describes the reflective process involved. And just as the mirror can give a flattering picture at times and a distorted, disappointing one at others, the self-concept tends to fluctuate in children, not really becoming relatively firmly fixed until age eighteen or so when the young adults have weathered adolescence – a time of uncertainty comparable to the terrible twos! Moreover, the picture is subdivided. While the self-concept is the picture itself, the self-esteem comes from the value the person gives to that picture. It is a global evaluation of one's own worth. It is the distance between the perceived self and the ideal self as shown in Figure 6.1.

Figure 6.1 Self-esteem

How does that come about? How does the child fix this important picture of himself? Harter (1990) tells us that the child's self-esteem is 'the product of two internal assessments or judgments'. Each child gauges some discrepancy between what he thinks he is like, and what he thinks he *ought* to be like, or what he would like to be. If there is just a short gap between the two, the child's self-esteem will be high. If, however, the distance is large, his self-esteem will be low. The child with dyspraxia may well feel inadequate or diminished if he thinks his clumsiness and social inadequacies are detrimental to his standing in the eyes of the important people around him, and indeed Harter points out the importance of the support children have from parents and friends. Now the dyspraxic child knows full well that he has difficulties, there is no use pretending they don't exist. But the children have to be sure that they are loved despite them, or better still loved even more because of them for many consider that they have let their parents down because they are unable to fulfil their hopes and dreams. They have to be told they are special possibly more often than other children because they are more liable to be hurt by uncaring or unknowing others. Children who feel that others like them will have a higher self-esteem than those that doubt others like them.

A further important point is that the children's self-concept is more likely to be affected by those they respect. If someone they don't approve of or don't care for offers a compliment or a diminishing comment they will not be particularly affected. They will be more able to shrug it off. They will more readily accept what people they look up to say as being true. These 'most important people' change at least temporarily. First parents, then teachers, then the peer group, then celebrities for fashion or lifestyle, appear as important role models.

Vulnerable children are hurt by the bullies but may not believe their taunts unless they are carried on for some time or unless other children join in. Then self-doubts are reinforced: 'They can't all be wrong, can they?' This is one reason why it is vital to stop bullying as fast as possible. Children with dyspraxia tend to take statements at face value, i.e. quite literally. Innuendoes are not understood and double meanings and sarcasm only confuse. Interestingly, children with an obvious or severe disability are not prone to be bullied – possibly this is why children with dyspraxia, a 'hidden handicap' (Kirby, 1999a), fare worse.

As they form their self-esteem, children set their own goals. The picture of the 'ideal' is not the same for every child. Some value academic work (intellectual goals) and wish to shine at that, while others value prowess in sports (perceptual-motor goals), or having good friends (social goals), even being able to be confident and 'cool' (emotional goals). When they anticipate, or experiences and interactions tell them that they are not going to achieve these goals at the level they would wish, then their self-esteem can take a nasty knock. Of course, nearly all children are the same in this respect, for not many achieve their early dreams of becoming a world champion racing driver or a prima ballerina. But when all things are equal, when children have no obvious limiting difficulties, realisation can take longer to set in and by this time other interests and opportunities may have taken their place.

Children with dyspraxia, however, are likely to realise sooner that their potential in several fields is reduced and that even with practice some goals are unobtainable. When children see themselves as failing to live up to their own goals, they need extra support and help. One would think that comfort statements, such as 'But look how good you are at your music, let's practise that and then you can play at the school concert', would help to compensate, but they only do so if the child values that activity himself – if that fits his framework of worthwhile things to do. Otherwise ideas are likely to be rejected and parents feel helpless, not knowing what to suggest.

Having said that, some children can show extreme commitment to achieving their preferred aim and overcome huge obstacles to do it, so parents have to try to assess the child's determination, try to provide resources (could outside agencies help?) that make achievement possible, or be ready with alternative suggestions which if possible link to the child's original idea of what he wants to do or be. Parents could seek out subtler ways of helping, to avoid causing the child stress – possibly making a tape recording of stories or plays, possibly devising computer games, possibly sending craft work in to *Blue Peter*, whatever will show the child he can succeed and so build the child's confidence.

A negative impact on self-esteem happens when children perceive that they have failed to live up to their family's expectations, even worse when they consider that their family's support is contingent upon them reaching some goal. And so the children are afraid to tell that they have poor marks or no friends or are being bullied or haven't a place in the school team. Even though these things may not be the children's fault, in their own eyes they are culpable. And of course, admitting them is so painful. Children will often be heard denying or disputing reality to try to retain a level of standing in their parents' eyes.

An important other component of the self-concept is 'body image', i.e. how children perceive their bodies and how nearly that matches their ideal – usually the 'cool', tall, slim, talented child. Children are surrounded by such images in magazines and in the media and if they don't see themselves as looking like that, their estimation of their own self-worth is diminished. This is particularly so if the children are by nature vulnerable and ambivalent about themselves. Unfortunately this can cause overeating for comfort. The children know that this will make the discrepancy worse and so feel guilty as well as greedy – or alternatively defiant, not caring – in other words they use denial strategies to help them cope, at least temporarily. This denial is a huge part of anorexia, which can be the way some children respond. This usually has an intrinsic psychological basis, which manifests itself in refusing to eat and being unable to recognise the degree of emaciation that occurs. Adults who are affected by this condition can weigh five stone and still believe themselves fat.

Peer pressure to conform has a big effect on self-esteem. Children who deviate from the group's unwritten norms are likely to feel inadequate. Labels and judgements from others play a vital role in the formation of the self-concept. To a very large extent 'we come to think of ourselves what others think of us' (Cole, 1991). This picture is derived from many sources, even unwitting remarks. Cole gives a good example. The child who comes home with a report card with threes or fours, and whose parents, thinking they are being supportive say, 'That's just fine - we didn't expect you to get ones,' is left with a clear message about the parents' expectations! Of course, 'Why didn't you get ones?' could have been even harder to handle! Dyspraxic children are likely to have widely diverging grades across the curriculum and parents will be able to point out that, 'That's you: the good ones, and that's your dyspraxia: the poorer ones', for surely sensitive teachers will have added a word of explanation? Perhaps they will have used alternative strategies as part of the assessment package, e.g. tape-recorded stories, sums written out so that the children have only to concentrate on the answers that have to be filled in. In this case, there may be no poor grades or negative-sounding comments at all. In Scotland's primary schools the system of levels with each child 'working towards' or 'attaining a level' rather than failing to achieve it, is accompanied by a teacher's statement, so the difficulties of reporting accurately and fully for dyspraxic children should be reduced.

The self-concept is gradually formed from these experiences but is not set in stone. It is responsive to changes in others' judgments and to the children's own successes. But once it is firmed up, it is relatively enduring, made more so by the fact that children will be likely to avoid activities that confirm a negative model: 'I can't do that, I'm no use at it'. While this seems sensible the children feel they have failed by not trying. Unfortunately, some children will generalise from this experience so that they feel they are no use, not only at the particular activity, but no use at all. This is a global self-concept: 'I'm good' or 'I'm a failure!' And once this idea has been reinforced by other 'failing' experiences – and the children may have selected these as a way to confirm the negative expectations they have of themselves – then depression may set in and remain through childhood and adolescence, even into adulthood. Counselling will try to effect change but the most vulnerable do not find it easy to believe what others say when lots of other circumstances have proved their own self-belief to be correct.

For the general population of children, the aim of education is to give them varied experiences so that they will build a balanced profile of their own abilities and have several successes to record. The idea is that they will select the 'best' and be proud of those achievements. Dyspraxic children who do not transfer learning from one situation to another will not relish this variety. Life is easier for them when they can choose what they want to do. For no one really has to play football or have neat handwriting or be able to sing? Perhaps we need to identify the essentials – the daily life skills – concentrate on teaching these as priority, then beyond that, let the children choose?

Enhancing children's self-concept

Giving praise

This book has emphasised the importance of giving positive feedback or praise especially to children with difficulties, so that their self-concept will be enhanced. But how is this best done? Do we simply tell children 'That's good' and leave it at that or are there helpful strategies to help us know what to do and ways that could be self-defeating?

Very young children will accept unrealistic praise. They will be delighted by any form of gratification. They move on quickly from one activity to the next and may not pause to think whether what they have produced merits what they have been told. But older children are likely to feel that unwarranted praise is demeaning. They are perfectly well able to evaluate their work and if this disappoints them, then they are not likely to accept someone else's judgment, except perhaps in a borderline case. What they may do is lose respect for the one who offers the praise. The point is that if children have any difficulties, their learning has to be structured into appropriate bite-size pieces so that with effort, the children can deserve praise. Children need genuine praise for progress that they can see. If teachers offer *realistic* praise the children know that their difficulties are understood.

Margaret Pope (1988), a head teacher of a school for children with learning difficulties, explains:

> I have been amazed at how well a child responds to an acceptance of his or her difficulties when this is coupled with a programme of positive activities that will lead to improvements. Telling a child he is good at something when as an intelligent human being he knows he's not, far from raising his self-esteem only reduces it.

This sentiment says 'be realistic but encouraging' and with dyspraxic children their intellectual capacity makes this perfectly possible. The intelligence, however, lets the children evaluate their 'product' against that of other children and frustration may result. Children have told me that 'Once I knew I had dyspraxia, I knew I wasn't stupid and that there would be things I could do well. It must be dreadful for children who can't manage anything at all really. How must they feel?' Reactions like this would seem to endorse labelling. Given a recognised label, the child then has a reason for his difficulties – one that has nothing to do with intelligence.

Example

One twelve-year-old explained, 'This smart-alec guy said to me, "Come on slow coach, what's keeping you?". I said "Dyspraxia" – he said, "What's that?" – I said, "Go and find out, you ninny!"' – which shows that, given a label, these children can retaliate, maybe not too politely either!

Dyspraxic children may well have difficulty pacing their effort. This means that they may not finish or may rush the last part spoiling the effect, just to be finished in time. This means that formative assessment with praise that also contains some ongoing guidance is the best way.

Example

'The colours you have chosen are really effective . . . your picture is coming on well. Remember to keep the design clear – don't spoil what you have done by making it fussy. You have 10 minutes to complete this part today. Let's set the timer. You'll need to put your painting on the drying screen before you tidy up the paints and water so get ready to finish this part for today and tomorrow you can do the next part.'

In this kind of scenario the children have praise and clear guidance about what to do next. The awareness of time problem is eased by the large egg timer, which the child will turn over after it is empty. This happening at five minutes lets the child know that half the time has gone. The organisation of subsequent events completed without undue haste, i.e. putting the painting aside before clearing away the water, will hopefully prevent disasters. A kindly 'buddy' nearby could be appointed to oversee these arrangements for the child if those instructions were too complex to be retained. Alternatively sequences of pictures can explain the sequence of events.

It is interesting and surprising to find that children with low self-esteem may rebuff praise, denying that they have made any improvement at all. If there is evidence of progress, they'll say, 'That was luck' rather than 'I did it better'. Are they so unused to praise that they can't believe others mean what they say? If their evaluation of themselves is 'fixed', this may be so. This means that parents and teachers have to spell out what progress entails for these children or else they may not realise they have succeeded. Without this support, they may deny they have made progress at all.

One fascinating piece of research by Gurney (1987) asked teachers to teach children to praise each other, but not in the way circle time does (because in my view that kind of praise can lose meaning because it is decontextualised) and being out of context causes children to say things like 'I like your hair' which doesn't hold much encouragement or in many cases doesn't even ring true. One way that was tried and evoked meaningful results is described now.

Example

Praising each other's work

First of all the children knew what was going to happen and they were allowed to choose the piece of work that was to be part of the game. There were no unexpected surprises. Children had time to plan and select. Then, two children (who were paired sensitively) had to look at each other's work closely and say one good thing about it. Sometimes this was, 'I can read it easily', a wonderful accolade for children who had difficulty with their writing skills or who often had letters out of order, or they made a comment about the imaginative content, e.g. 'That's good about Bob (the dog in one child's story), it makes me want to read on to find out if he gets out of the cave'. The comment might also be about the vocabulary: 'You have used some of the words we learned at drama, that's great'.

This kind of peer praise was found to be really effective. The children accepted praise from their peers. Moreover the activity reinforces the teaching points for all of the children and the teacher has a chance to find the points that were important to each child. All the children can join in an activity like this and when the criteria concern 'good story lines' rather than neatness, the dyspraxic child's story can very often be the one read out to the class. As different children give their feedback, the teachers can see if the children choose to use the criteria that they themselves would apply and this can be very revealing as to whether the teaching points have been taken on board. Teachers who have tried this tell me this approach works best when it happens quite infrequently, when the children have had some advance notice and when they themselves have discreetly checked that the pieces of work have the qualities the assessing children can identify. If these can be 'new' things, (e.g. 'Has anyone found a poem without rhyming words?') this prevents repetition and keeps the activity alive.

The arrows in Figure 6.2 show that when the aims of the teaching or the activity are consistently met then interest and motivation are lost. Perhaps this is why golf stays as a long time challenge – even the experts cannot have a perfect round each time and although a hole in one is possible, it is particularly elusive. And even when golfers are experts, new challenges arise when a different course or different weather conditions create an unfamiliar environment. Perhaps this explains why playground games such as hopscotch or skipping are all the rage, then just as suddenly they disappear. The children who can do them well get unremitting positive feedback which loses impact and those who have never managed abandon the game anyway. In classrooms, having varying levels of praise given intermittently seems to be the way to keep children on task. Teachers have to be psychologists too!

But of course praise need not be verbal from another person. Satisfaction in the activity is a kind of praise in itself – if not for progress then certainly for commitment.

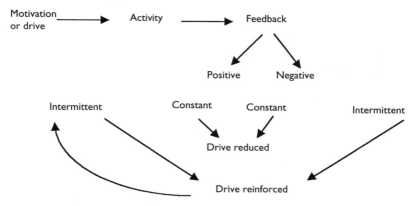

Figure 6.2 The drive reduction theory

The importance of practice

> ### Example
>
> #### Coral
>
> One little girl, Coral, had severe perceptual-motor problems. Her balance was so poor that she often tipped off her seat. When she sat for any length of time she collapsed into herself and she did her writing leaning flat on her desk with her head turned to face the page. I was asked to try to find out what was wrong and so I carried out an assessment using a number of 'fun-to-do' activities. Coral, at twelve years old, couldn't manage any of these with any degree of success until it came to catching a ball. She could catch from any angle, even with one hand, even with her non-preferred hand (although she had little sense of hand dominance). She had found balancing possible by having her feet wide apart and intermittently leaning against a wall. Her ball skills provided a genuine opportunity for congratulations. Coral explained the reason why: 'Well at home, every night I play against the wall. It's great fun!'

This was a lovely illustration of the effectiveness of sustained and regular practice. The words 'sustained' – for 15 minutes at a time – and 'regular' – four or five times each week – are the critical ones here. Obviously Coral was having positive feedback from this activity and it had not yet reached saturation point possibly because she often set herself new challenges such as having jingles which meant the ball activity had to be rhythmical – even trying two balls, or in Coral's parlance, 'doublies!' (For further activities see Appendices 2–4.)

But how do parents and teachers encourage children who have no interest in some fundamental skill to practise it? Long-term goals are not effective motivators. Delayed gratification is not usually appreciated, so the activity has to be broken down into manageable parts. If this still doesn't motivate the child, is it possible to relate the competencies that are being practised to something the child would like to do better? Walking along a bench in the gym can be pretty boring and not give much incentive to 'push the head high', but if the child understands that this is an important way to help him balance and that 'looking ahead, not down at your feet' is really 'a practice for pedalling your bike' because 'when you are riding your bike, you can't look down or you'll not see where you are going', then the child might be more inclined to try. And so the key factors in successful practice are to do it:

- in short spells – 15 minutes or so at a time but four or five times each week;
- regularly – two or three times a day, possibly at the same time of day for children with severe difficulties; with explanations why the exercises are important so that the child:
  a   understands how best to cooperate, and
  b   appreciates the possible outcome, i.e. what 'other things' he will be enabled to do.

Chapter 7

Practical considerations for parents and teachers

When parents of young people with dyspraxia were asked to say what criteria they would use to choose a school, they said:

- a warm welcoming atmosphere, a caring ethos;
- staff genuinely believing in inclusion and valuing each child;
- friendly staff – people who have time to listen and who want to understand the condition and how to support my child;
- a uniform of polo shirts and pull-on sweaters – no ties, no laces, no buttons;
- near home if possible but more importantly, away from a busy road;
- classes that already have children with learning differences;
- no homework.

These were the key criteria. League tables were not important to any of the parents. 'We can cope with lots of things', the parents explained, 'if the teachers will only be allowed time to listen to us explaining the positive moves we have found helpful. This is so important but often professionals believe they have to find everything out for themselves.'

This of course may be because the child at home and at school can conduct themselves very differently, not because of any unwillingness to communicate with the parents or wish to ignore their expertise.

The practical strategies listed in this chapter have come from preceding chapters where the implications of children's difficulties have been explained. And just as individual children have different symptoms of dyspraxia with different levels of severity, the strategies to help them must be individually selected too. Parents and teachers know their children well. They know what kinds of help children are likely to accept and what kinds of intervention could make them feel worse. If children even know that everything possible is being done and that people are doing their best, they are more likely to accept that they must play a part in trying things out and sharing their thoughts about the helpfulness or otherwise of the strategies that have been tried. Communication between parents and teachers is imperative if the children are not to be confused by different signals, different value systems and different expectations.

Advice to parents, teachers and policy makers

The education authorities must play their part in helping children with dyspraxia. Teachers do not have endless time or unlimited resources. So the authorities should provide special equipment such as inclined boards for reading and writing. These make a huge difference to the children – they are not very expensive and they just have to be supplied, or else some children will have major unnecessary difficulties. Inclusion doesn't just mean everyone together, it implies a humane learning environment where children with special needs have them recognised and where resources are such that the best opportunity for learning is provided. While parents should not have to pay for any resources, they may wish to do so if help from the authorities is delayed. They would then remain as the property of the child, going home at weekends or holidays. On the other hand, inclined boards and wobble boards can be improvised quite cheaply and if there are parents who are joiners or have DIY skills, perhaps they would be prepared to help. Class fundraising could also help the other children to contribute ideas/songs/pictures for an exhibition and it is good for them to play a positive part in rallying round to help their less fortunate friend.

If the child needs to take tests for school reasons, he will be entitled to have more time than other children, to have questions or maps blown up (and this may necessitate a bigger desk to support them) or to have a scribe. Well before the test, the child needs to practise with items in similar enlarged sizes and with someone scribing for him. Several ways of helping the child gauge the passing of time may also be required. Any test will be harrowing enough without surprises.

Practical strategies to help

1   At school
2   Getting ready for school
3   At home

At school

The learning environment

- Ensure that the children have an uninterrupted view of the board.
- Remove distractors whenever possible – if not, make sure dyspraxic children are away from problems such as noise from computers, children passing, trees at windows, noises from the dining hall or other classrooms, in fact anything that will distract them and spoil their concentration.
- It would be an advantage for such children to be seated a little distance from others, if the child cannot bear his personal space to be invaded.
- Check that the children can sit comfortably, well supported in suitable chairs. Hard chairs with metal legs tend to tip easily and this makes balance very difficult. If balance is a problem, sitting on the floor is not easy – it may even be painful. Allow the children to lean against a support and don't expect them to sit too long in one position.
- Desks should be at elbow height. Small children benefit from a step (two telephone directories) if the desks are too high. Dangling legs pull the body forward over the desk and as they don't give support, this makes control of pencils or shifting papers difficult.
- Give an inclined board for writing and reading. This eases tracking from the board to the jotter when writing. The angle also eases pressure on the wrist and allows the pen or pencil to flow. The inclined board also helps reading because the eyes are less likely to jump over letters. For children who need to press hard to obtain feedback from their proprioceptors, avoid pencils that break easily.
- Allow children to try out various pencil sizes to see which suits their individual grip. Triangular grips help some but not all children.

- Check that any overhead light does not glare or reflect on the children's work. This exacerbates visual difficulties and can be very irritating for children who already have difficulty focusing and retaining their place on the page.
- Use a large-scale laminated timetable to point out the routine of the day. Have symbols for PE kit, e.g. a ball, for 'homework given out', e.g. a closed book; for 'homework in', perhaps an open jotter full of writing. Symbols can also be used for letters home and for when they are to come back. All of these and others, which the children can choose, alert those with poor planning to the days when special things have to be done. The timetable has to be big so that it does not become cluttered and confusing to the child it is meant to help.
- Colour coding is very helpful and has many applications. Colour coding pegs in the cloakroom, trays, jotters, even pens, pencils and rubbers help children to identify their own things and saves squabbling. If the child chooses red as his colour, have him in the red group in class.
- Dots on pages to show the child where to begin and end are sometimes necessary, or if children have to do alternate sums on a page, it can be quicker to colour code them than to replan a worksheet.
- Whenever possible keep a strict routine, for example always send letters home on a Friday. Then, even if the children forget, the parents know to check schoolbags and retrieve the letters before they are covered in mud off the games shoes or the juice spilt from the tumbler that has lost its lid. This avoids parents missing occasions such as parents' night and wanting another appointment – so this extra preparation can pay off in the long run!
- Make sure the children with dyspraxia have extra tissues or wet wipes to ease visits to the toilet. And when they wish to go, don't ask them to delay. They may get little warning. Give them extra time, especially if buttons have to be undone. On the other hand they may just forget to come back – running water has a fascination for many children, so keep an eye out for them and make sure they aren't gone too long.
- Perhaps the classroom assistant could be earmarked to keep tabs thus ensuring the child can undertake routine jobs like taking a message to another teacher. This would give the child's self-esteem a huge boost. But remember, unsupervised, he may not return. As one teacher exclaimed, 'I couldn't let Ewan go with a message … he'd never come back!'

Teaching

- Try to minimise what the children have to do without taking the responsibility away – help the children plan and organise but don't do the whole job for them. Gauge what the child can manage with support, and leave appropriate challenges.
- Identify the ways the child learns best: visually, 'hands-on' or through listening to instructions. Try to present the key learning issues in ways that would be sensitive to these preferred modes.
- Organise the learning in short spells and give time to relax in between. Experiment with having music playing. For some children this helps concentration, while others find this distracting, so once again be guided by the child's response.
- Reduce the number of items, sums or sentences the child has to complete so that he may finish at the same time as the other children. Ask the parents or classroom assistant to scribe stories or write out sums in advance, so that the child has only to work out

the answers. And as the child's planning improves, give him small responsibilities such as giving out worksheets to his own table, anything that will boost his self-esteem.

- Only give essential homework as the child will be tired and will be unable to complete it well. Understand if he explains that he was too tired. Allow him to tape a story rather than have to write it.
- At the start of each lesson try to provide a recap of some sort. Remember, these children can have short-term memory problems and this may cause them to forget what has been taught in an earlier lesson. For the same reason dyspraxic children need extra repetition of key learning issues, which can be through word banks or through giving the children access to books to remind them of what has gone before.
- Give stars for progress by all means and praise whenever praise is merited, in line with each child's ability and effort. Do not offer rewards 'for doing it more neatly' or ask the child to 'do it again'. If the work is illegible, then the child will be able to read it to you tomorrow when he is not so tired.
- Use traffic lights to signal basic instructions:

  - red – 'Wait in your seat, I'm busy';
  - yellow – 'Time to tidy up' or 'Get ready';
  - green – 'I am ready to see you now' or 'Begin now!'

  This prevents children approaching at inappropriate times and having to be rebuffed.
- Use masking tape to fix the child's papers to the desk as this frees his two hands for other jobs.
- Use large coloured arrows to give directions to the hall, the toilets, the library or the cloakrooms. These help children who are confused in corridors, and if the places are named, this also helps the poor readers.
- Use kitchen timers so that the children have a visual picture of how much time is left. If the twisting action needed to make the timer work is difficult (two hands working together at the midline) then a large egg timer is fun and does the job just as well. The child may of course prefer to watch the sand trickling through rather than working – it could provide a distraction. Kitchen timers can indicate the amount of time left to finish a job or be used for 'time-out', i.e. times to relax for a moment or to regain control after a mishap (only for pupils!).
- Remember that these children take things literally. 'Pull your socks up' means just that. Above all, remember that children with dyspraxia may be impetuous and have poor self-preservation skills. I always say to my students, 'It's bad enough if the children can't read, but if they get hurt, that's far more serious'. So, if children say they can swim, check that's true before allowing them in deep water, for they may not realise they are out of their depth.
- On trips out, they may dart into the road without stopping to check there is no traffic. They may hear surrounding noises, but not recognise the distance and direction of approaching cars and they are so anxious not to be last! They will get lost unless there are clear instructions, but let the children practise reading them before the actual outing.
- A last word is a plea for you to remember these children have a disability. It is with them all day every day. It is not easy to have dyspraxia or for families to live with it. Children often feel they have let their families down by being like this. They are anxious not to let

their school down, too. In a supportive environment they are sure to be trying just as hard as they can because they are clever children who know you are trying to help.

Getting ready for school: equipment

- Schoolbag – firmly attach a large, colourful, personal motif to help identification especially if the bag spends the day in a large box of other schoolbags. Have name and contact phone number prominently displayed inside the flap.
- Choose a roomy bag with two front pockets. Always use these for the same things, e.g. pencil case in one pocket, letters home, bus passes, tissues, wet wipes (personal things) in the other. This makes packing and checking easier and quicker.
- Choose Velcro fastenings or easy clips.
- Inside the flap have a laminated timetable – a smaller version of the one at home and at school.
- Pencil case – a large see-through pencil case can have a list of contents fixed inside so that they can be checked. Don't have too many pens, etc. If there are any special instructions, e.g. 'Go to Gran's from school today', a card in the pencil case can give a reminder and free the child from trying to retain that information all day. NB Always remember to take the card out once it has served its purpose, or the child may carry out the instructions another day. He may not be sure that he visited yesterday and go again!
- Lunch box – packed lunches are a good idea if using a knife and fork is difficult.
- Check whether the box opens and closes easily.
- Wrap sandwich in foil, not cling film. Fillings such as cheese are easier to handle than those which make the bread soggy. Lettuce can be difficult to chew for children with poor muscle tone in the mouth. Check biscuits can be unwrapped easily – some are nearly impossible.
- Drinks – have a wide-necked stable bottle, not one that tips easily. If the child will tolerate water, this makes less mess on clothes or floors if it is spilt. Avoid cartons that need straws pushed through or tops torn off. (Two-handed coordination may be difficult and the child will squeeze the carton against the body. Then the juice spurts out and makes a mess.)
- Wet wipes – provide these to clean hands, ease toilet visits and mop spills.
- PE kit – this should be as roomy as the child will allow, to ease changing quickly. Elastic waists and Velcro fastenings make a huge difference. Provide a plastic bag for carrying dirty equipment home and if shoes are left in school, remember to check sizes as the child grows.
- School uniform – avoid laces and buttons and ties if at all possible. Have Velcro everywhere. Arrange for the teacher to have spare pants if accidents should happen. The child may wait too long before asking to go out and poor muscle control in the bladder means he is caught short. If the toilets are some way off, the child may underestimate the time needed to get there or in a panic forget where to go.

At home

- Parents advise, 'Always get up early. Allow time for three things to go wrong. They always do. If the day begins in a rush, somehow the whole day goes wrong. Use lists with picture cues for the wee ones. Show the children that you are using them, for this helps the children to realise that they are useful for grown-ups too. They also help the children become more independent. Give them special routine jobs to do, but remember they have little sense of time – allow plenty or everyone will fall out.'

- Keep the environment simple. A child who has difficulty with perceptual-motor tasks is best within a quiet, non-patterned environment. Plain carpets mean that shoes and dropped items can be easily found and plain walls mean that lists can stand out. This helps the morning speed!
- A large timetable is also a good idea as it reminds the child of the things he needs and what is happening that day. If it is laminated, then markings can be wiped off when routines change.
- Establish a routine. Give all the children small jobs to do such as setting the table or helping to clear away. Keep the job the same till it has been mastered.
- Devise strategies so that the dyspraxic child can be as independent as possible: decant breakfast cereal into a plastic box. This means the child can help himself. Don't fill jugs of juice too full or there will be spills.
- Have plastic beakers that are light but firm.
- Use sliced bread so that everyone can make their own toast.
- Make sure the chairs are at the correct height. Kitchen stools are not advised as they tip when the child leans over. They are also easily knocked over if the child is one who bumps into things.
- Have a large non-digital clock in a prominent place or set the kitchen timer for 30/20/10 minutes before leaving.
- Make lists of routines to help the child get organised.

<table>
<tr><td>

Example 1

Bedroom wall list

1　Toilet
2　Wash hands and face
3　Go down for breakfast
4　Clean teeth
5　Get dressed (a separate number chart may help the order of putting on clothes)
6　Fold pyjamas
7　Tidy room

</td><td>

Example 2

Front door list
Have you got your:

1　Schoolbag
2　Pencil case
3　Lunch box
4　Homework (Fridays)
5　PE kit (Mondays)
6　Coat and scarf?

Have a good day, love mum.

</td></tr>
</table>

Mums say, 'I find lists help, but we never seem to reach the last item!'

And when all of this seems just too much, we need to listen and remember what Gurney (1987) decreed. He said:

Teachers and parents praise yourselves. Say out loud what you have achieved today. Tell others. For sure, they could not do as well!

Chapter 8

Transition to secondary school

Adolescence in youngsters with dyspraxia: notes for parents and teachers

Example

Lisa, whose twelve-year-old son Alex has dyspraxia

'Alex's dyspraxia is severe and on really bad days when sleeping has been difficult, he doesn't go to school. As he gets older he falls further and further behind. He's an intelligent boy and the school has tried to accommodate him; I have no complaints at all, but he is finding secondary school really challenging. If he misses days, the youngsters who befriended him find other things to do and he loses track of what they are doing in class. It's a nightmare for the family and so much worse for him. I think we are on the brink of depression so I am wondering about home schooling with tutors but the cost is horrendous. I wish there was a special school for youngsters who are intellectually bright even if they lack other skills.'

Lisa's account shows that transition to secondary school can be particularly stressful for students with dyspraxia. They must leave their relatively sheltered primary where they and their families are well known; where routines and timetables are well established; where books and resources are in well rehearsed places; where distances and directions in school and going home are reassuringly familiar and above all where their individual profiles of strengths and difficulties have been appreciated and supported by all the staff in a small community. Now the future holds a new daunting set of challenges, which in the students' eyes at least must be met all at once. Expectations of what the children will do independently are suddenly much greater and of course this is matched by many more opportunities to fail. And all of this happens at a time when adolescence is kicking in, when hormonal changes and growth spurts can appear too early or too late or even when they are timely, they can cause disquiet. Little wonder that 'the youngster with dyspraxia feels even more unsure, frustrated and isolated than ever before' (Taylor, 2007).

The sense of isolation can be heightened by other children eagerly anticipating the transition in the certainty that they will be able to cope with the new, complex demands. Conversations often focus on the real or imagined negative things that will happen there – or these may be the only ones the students with dyspraxia hear. Stories about strict teachers 'who don't put up with latecomers' or 'who insist on neat work' terrify and dismay children who find meeting deadlines challenging. In addition, many adolescent youngsters find it difficult to communicate fears especially if they anticipate they may sound silly to others without the difficulties dyspraxia brings. So they brood and may become depressed. However, comfort can come from the finding that once the students settle, the greater variety of subjects and the varied personnel can provide positive feedback. This is very encouraging. Sharing this with the young people should help their self-esteem.

So what can be done? The chapter firstly outlines some practical suggestions for parents and teachers; then issues of sexuality will be discussed.

Suggestions for parents

- If you have a choice of schools try to visit when the students are present and note the ambience. Your child must feel valued and safe. Look at the other students – do they look relaxed and at ease? Look at the discipline at break times for young people charging along corridors could alarm and distress those with dyspraxia. Look at the welcome notices. Are they newly in place or tattered from having hung there too long? Are children from ethnic minorities given their special welcome? Are there photos of children in wheelchairs or other minority groups given pride of place? This all suggests inclusion and that all children will be seen as unique individuals.

- Then consider the length of time the staff have offered you to explain your child's profile of difficulties. Even if they have had children with dyspraxia before, these other students' profile of abilities and difficulties will not be the same as yours. You need time. Request a thirty-minute appointment well ahead of time so that the staff can plan your visit. Take a list outlining your child's strengths as well as his difficulties and assure the school that you are anxious to cooperate in every way.

- Look at the signposting in the school. Are directions to classrooms and toilets clear? Young people shouldn't need to ask others where to go, for this can be overwhelmingly difficult and a source of great stress especially if some prankster tells them the wrong way. Even if this is clear, ensure students are allowed to leave the class to visit the loo. Often new situations can irritate bladders and queues at break times can mean missed opportunities. Having to rush can also cause accidents.

- Ask how many young people are in each class and what provision is made for teenagers with dyspraxia when they have practical sessions, when e.g. they have to handle scientific or mathematical equipment, e.g. glass pipettes or compasses.

- If your child is easily tired, ask if he needs to undertake all of the lessons each day. No one really needs ten subjects and if your child has physiotherapy programmes or simply gets tired easily, then cutting one is an obvious solution. Although PE is very important, team games can cause so much stress that the benefit is often lost. Added to this, remembering rules – especially difficult when the teams change sides and play the other way and having to change into sports gear can harass the young people beyond endurance.

- Ask if there is easy access to computers and if a laptop is available for your child's use – or if he has a personal one, will all staff allow its use? Many children find these easier and quicker that writing longhand and having one allows children to keep up with the rest of the class. If writing longhand is required, then the heights of the desks need to be checked so that the students don't have to slouch or stretch.

- Ask if there is a specially designated classroom assistant for at least part of the day. This is vital if your child is significantly affected by his dyspraxia. A good idea is to ask for an appointment with the SENCO and make a list of things to ask. Also note down what has been said at the meeting because remembering the details can be tricky in an emotional situation and it is important for the child to be as well informed and as independent as possible. If the student is not present at the meeting asking if it can be taped can let him hear a friendly voice and minimise his fears.

- Ask about other young people with dyspraxia who made the transition one year earlier. How did they fare? Were their difficulties recognised and allowances made? Even if this was done well, staff have to know that students with dyspraxia are not the same and that they will have a different profile of needs. Also that youngsters may be less willing to share these – in fact they may insist they are managing well and explode when they get home.

- If you manage to contact older students who have attended the school, ask them to share their experiences with your child and to allay his fears. They will know where to find the SENCO or Year Head who will take responsibility for all the children with learning differences. They know how available these busy people are and when it is easiest to contact them. It is best if the pupil with dyspraxia can meet this person before term begins so that any potential barriers are broken down. These older students will also know what provision is made e.g. providing lockers for students who find it difficult to carry heavy books. This is really important because often children with dyspraxia, having made 'memory slips' before, will insist on carrying all of their books in case they have brought the wrong ones on the wrong day. Knowing that most are safely in school with reserve pencils and bus money can reduce a great deal of stress caused by having to remember.

- Children with a range of difficulties may well be allowed into school slightly earlier than the others to avoid the bustle at bell time or there may be a buddy system to support them in the first days. It is also a time when children with learning differences can meet each other to compare notes and even if they are not in the same teaching group, there will be a known face in the corridor or the lunch queue.

- Make at least two holiday visits to the school to familiarise your child with directions in and around the building. A cooperative janitor, contacted ahead of time, may allow children to find their classrooms and to practise going from the front door to the hall and then the class or whatever the usual procedure is. Then the student can be independent of following others around for nothing is worse than dreading not knowing where to go. Anticipating being lost can spoil the keenest student's concentration. A simple map with indicators, e.g. a drawn fire extinguisher that is near the entrance to the art room, can be a great resource.

- These visits allow practising the route home too. If memorising is difficult, draw a map of the outside of the building showing school gates and bus stops with times of buses if the children travel this way. They can be reassured by knowing that if they miss one bus another will be along shortly. Write the number of the bus clearly with the times in their wallet. This should also have the home phone number and any mobile number that could prove helpful, especially if the student is likely to get flustered.

- Ask for a copy of the class timetable and duplicate several of these. Separate the master into strips for each day and make sure they are changed as routine in the evenings. Ask what PE kit is required, buy it early and substitute Velcro for buttons whenever possible. Practise changing into these at home and ask if a T-shirt can replace a shirt or blouse on sports days.

- Prepare a list of the things the child can do well alongside his difficulties. The list is proof that you have shared concerns and helps parents to be less emotional while explaining. Ask the SENCO how other subject teachers are informed of the child's learning difference and if/how they adapt their lessons. Let them know that this information will help you to support their way of doing things at home and prevent the child being confused by different methods.
- Ask how school information is communicated home and if your child has difficulty remembering, ask if you might phone the school if a problem arises. Knowing a secretary's name can make contact easier. The school will have your number on file for emergencies. It is helpful to give a second contact number if possible.
- This done, encourage the children to take pride in preparing for the new adventure – but quietly oversee the organisation of books and lunch boxes each day. Colour coding books and jotters for each subject helps organisation and saves time and energy too.
- If the child resents articles such as lunch boxes being named, then affix a logo to ease identification.
- Check what equipment is acceptable. Velcro fastenings save tying laces; if see-through pencil cases are OK fine, if not then a small one on view while the other that contains daily reminders, a good quality eraser and sharpener (with a reservoir to catch shavings) can be hidden in the larger case. Having these loose in the schoolbag can cause flustered searching and damaged jotters, etc.

The secret is to know the details of the day and to do whatever it takes to reduce stress. But also remember that many other children have difficulties too. Also many children over react when they come into the safety of their home environment. Incidents can get blown out of proportion so parents should try to keep calm and have some quiet time before the inevitable question, 'What did you do at school today?' spoils the mood. Trying to interrupt with 'That sounds really interesting' might also refute any claims of the work being 'dead boring' – a usual teenagers' cry.

It is important to differentiate too between the difficulties that come from dyspraxia and other teenage angst!

Indicators for teachers

Students with dyspraxia are outwardly no different from any other but they have significant problems that need understanding and tolerance. They have average or even above average intelligence but will tire easily (due to poor habituation and sleeping problems) and this will exacerbate their lack of movement control.

It is really important to build an ability profile for each student and no two will exhibit the same pattern of difficulties. There may be co-occurring problems that occur with dyspraxia, e.g. tics or explosions of sound that are more to do with another difficulty, in this case Tourette's syndrome. This may cause more obvious distress than the dyspraxic difficulties but should not be allowed to mask them. Both have to be considered.

Indicators of dyspraxia

- General clumsiness: 'floppy posture' and a strange gait with the student showing poor balance and control.

- Movements that appear awkward; slowness in responding to instructions. The student may be summoning strength or rehearsing instructions and this takes a moment or two.
- A tendency to slouch. This is due to poor muscle tone not giving the body enough support, not laziness or disinterest in the lesson.
- An inability to sit still, especially if the chair is too high to allow legs to hold steady on the floor. This is due to a vestibular sense (sense of balance) that is not functioning well. Specially designed seats, available from physiotherapy centres or child and family centres, that allow some movement can help. Then the proprioceptors, i.e. nerve endings all over the body are stimulated to give the student a sense of where he is in space.
- Confusion in laterality; pupils changing hands to complete a written task rather than attempting to cross the midline.
- Poorly developed organisational skills. This means that all sequencing activities, e.g. in writing essays or mathematical equations could be difficult.
- Lack of awareness of time – students have no clear understanding of '10 minutes to finish' and need visual reminders. Some will not be able to repeat the days of the week or even the seasons in the correct order so reminders are essential.
- Many are extra sensitive to levels of heat/cold and are readily distracted by movements and/or sounds in the environment.
- Poor short-term memories make over-learning necessary. This is a source of much frustration when instructions have to be repeated and earlier learning is forgotten.
- Sometimes the children's difficulties cause them to be loners – tolerant friends who understand the condition and see the student underneath are a great help. With the parents' permission it is a good idea to explain the difficulties to a trustworthy group so that support can be shared. Then one willing youngster does not feel besieged by always having to be responsible.
- Students with dyspraxia often have difficulty copying from the board as lines of text run into one another. Providing an on-desk sheet of instructions is very helpful.
- Above all contact the parents, perhaps sharing a diary so that communication is quick and key moments are not forgotten. It also helps to ensure that both parties offer the same kind of support. Then notes from home to school (e.g. that a student has had a bad night and is struggling to cope), or from school to home (e.g. that a child's behaviour showed that his medication should be checked), can be shared calmly with a sense of trust, both parties recognising that each was working to support the child.
- All the work home should be dated to prevent duplication and unnecessary stress.

Coping with the changes at adolescence

Adolescence is a time of uncertainty for most youngsters and more so for those with dyspraxia. Sexuality is not only about sex although this is important; it is about the students' feelings and awareness of their own bodies and how this affects their self-esteem. It covers how they relate to other young people and the new social freedom that adolescence brings. It is about how to respond to others who may ask them to share inappropriate behaviour.

Some young people with dyspraxia will sail through puberty, others will be too anxious to please and not recognise when invitations may lead to danger. There can be an immaturity that makes it difficult to explain e.g. why visitors can be invited to see toddlers in the bath but not young adolescents – without suggesting that there is anything shameful in one's body. Such explanations have to be done a little at a time and with a great deal of tact. It is important that the youngsters learn about privacy in a matter of fact 'this is what we do' kind of way. Keeping a channel of communication open is vital. If others who want them to join them in abusive behaviour approach dyspraxic youngsters they have to know what to do and say. Giving advice e.g. 'If you feel uncomfortable, ask them to wait till you have discussed this at school or at home', can be a life saving mantra. This delaying tactic will deter any 'chancer' while not spoiling a friendship if the offer was all right. But this level of sharing will only be possible if puberty and the freedoms of adolescence have been approached in a matter of fact way. Youngsters have to know that while most contemporaries are kind and considerate, others can be cruel and mislead them. Telling them to wait is a good way to be safe.

MATURING AT THE 'RIGHT TIME'

Awareness that other students are experiencing bodily changes too can be a source of comfort – more so if they are developing at the same time as the youngster with dyspraxia. Again they may need to be reassured: 'It happens to everyone – me too – you are just the same as everyone else and if we share feelings and discuss things when we are on our own at home, then we can take all the changes in our stride'.

SHAPE AND SIZE

One of the most striking changes at adolescence is the growth spurt that changes the proportions of the youngster. During this time boys especially may add 3–6 inches in height for several years. And the hands and feet grow first making the ordinary teenager awkward and 'all hands and feet' – more so for the dyspraxic student who has more difficulty controlling his limbs anyway. The trunk is usually the last part to mature hence the 'gangliness' of the adolescent.

MUSCLES

During adolescence, muscle fibres become much thicker and stronger. This should help the dyspraxic youngster. By age 17, boys tend to be three times stronger than girls. Such a difference in muscle mass is down to the production of hormones. This is where activity helps. Swimming is especially good for the water supports the body while providing the resistance that strengthens the limbs. It can also be enjoyed as an individual sport without any fear of letting the team down.

FAT

Fat is significant in the physical make up of pre-adolescent girls and boys and as puberty approaches it causes much angst. In a study by Smoll and Schultz (2006) they found that between ages 13 and 17, the percentage of body fat amongst girls rose from 21–28 per cent while for boys it dropped from 16–14 per cent. So during and after puberty, the proportion of fat increases in girls while strength increases in boys.

INCREASE IN SIZE OF ORGANS

The heart and lungs also increase in size at adolescence and the heart rate drops. All of these changes are more marked in boys, influencing both their strength and endurance.

Table 8.1 Major hormones involved in physical growth and development

Gland	Hormone(s) secreted	Influence on growth
Thyroid gland	Thyroxine	Brain development; growth. Over- or under-production of the hormone must be medically treated
Adrenal gland	Adrenal androgen	Pubertal changes, particularly secondary sex characteristics in girls
Testes (in boys)	Testosterone	Vital in formation of male genitals prenatally; also triggers the primary and secondary sex characteristics in boys Girls have testosterone too but in much smaller amounts
Ovaries (in girls)	Oestrogen	Development of the menstrual cycle and breast development in girls
Pituitary gland – the 'leader' of the endocrine orchestra	Growth hormone	Controls the rate of growth and stimulates other glands to secrete their hormones

Development of sexual maturity

The hormonal changes of puberty stimulate the development of full sexual maturity. This means that changes in the primary sex characteristics (i.e. the testes and penis in boys and the ovaries, vagina and uterus in girls) are occurring, while secondary characteristics, i.e. breast development in girls and voice change and beard growth in boys accompany the growth of body hair in both sexes. For all children in all cultures the sequence of progress through these changes is the same although the timing can vary from child to child, causing much misery if things happen 'too early' or 'too late'.

IN GIRLS

First menstruation: this typically happens two years after the first apparent body changes (breast development and pubic hair). However, early periods do not mean sexual maturity for in the first ten or so months no ovum is produced. Periods are irregular, making preparation difficult, especially for girls with dyspraxia who may have difficulty remembering times when periods are due anyway. They should always be prepared so that they are not taken unawares and embarrassed in class. A pretty, waterproof cosmetic bag can hide supplies and be private.

These girls need particular support and reminders of how to cope, e.g. to change pads at every visit to the loo and how and where to dispose of used sanitary items. Providing cleansing wipes is especially useful when girls find changing and keeping fresh difficult. Some girls will try to share their experiences and any discomfort vociferously and adults have to explain that certain times for doing this, e.g. during lessons, are taboo.

IN BOYS

In boys the peak of the growth spurt comes later than the other aspects of sexual growth. The development of beard and the lowering of the voice comes quite late in the developmental sequence. The timing of the production of viable sperm is difficult to determine – it is mooted as being between ages 12 and 14 but it also seems to be ahead of the final part of the growth spurt.

Adolescent boys with dyspraxia are likely to have difficulty learning to shave because this involves two hands doing different things, crossing the midline of the body while looking in a mirror and possibly balancing precariously. Simple things, e.g. lowering the mirror so that the boy can sit and making sure that there is no rush can help. But they will need support just as the girls do.

Family relationships

Bringing up an adolescent can be traumatic enough without the frustrations of dyspraxia adding angst. Many youngsters with dyspraxia are intellectually ready to be more independent but their parents worry that their poor motor skills, memory and possible social problems will leave them vulnerable. Teenagers have two apparently contradictory roles in their relationships with their parents. The first is to be autonomous and that often causes conflict; the second is to maintain close family ties. Parents may well consider that the first is taking over yet research into lasting parent/child discord shows that only four per cent of children break away for good. When children have a specific learning difference like dyspraxia, there may be an element of blame emanating even covertly from parent to teenagers, e.g. mums crying or even just implying, 'Despite all I've done for you ...' (and this will have been a great deal more than if dyspraxia had not been present) – and from teenagers to parents – 'I didn't ask to have dyspraxia and as it's hereditary, whose fault is it anyway?' and this can fuel any calm discussion. Gecas and Seff (1990) suggest that adolescence may actually be more traumatic for the parents because of their diminishing control and their worries for the teenagers' safety.

Steinberg (1988) suggests that although this time can be really distressing and seem never ending, especially when both parties are tired of the struggle, far from being a negative event, it may be developmentally necessary and even healthy. It is a natural part of the separation process. The teenager is trying out independence while still sheltered by the family. In fact doctors have suggested that teenagers' poor behaviour at home is a compliment! It shows they are secure enough to release feelings of anxiety, knowing in their hearts that the status quo within the family will endure. In the main, teenagers remained firmly attached to home.

Levitt's research: a task to try

Levitt *et al.* (1993) gave different groups of children aged seven, ten and fourteen in different cultures a set of concentric circles. In the centre circle they were asked to write the names of 'people who are closest to you – who you love the most and who love you the most'. In the next circle going outwards the children had to nominate 'people who are not quite as close as those you named in the centre circle but still really important people' and in the outer ring they had to list 'people who were important without necessarily caring for them'. Later they were asked to describe the kind of support each group offered.

Levitt found that in all age groups and in all cultures parents' names appeared in the centre circle. Even fourteen-year-olds rarely placed friends in this position but they did acknowledge the importance of the support friends gave. However the results clearly showed the importance of parents continuing to provide a secure base. They stayed central – a finding that offers comfort when parents ask themselves, most often unnecessarily, 'Where did we go wrong?'.

Research into stages of puberty and the link with teenage aggression (Steinberg 1988) found that visible pubertal changes, especially the onset of menstruation in the girls, changes parents' attitudes towards their youngsters. Fears of teenage pregnancies or drug usage or 'getting into the wrong crowd' replace what on reflection seemed simple worries, e.g. playground spats or growth spurts and spots! So what kind of parenting style will be most likely to survive this tempestuous time?

Parenting styles

Baumrind's (1972) typology of parenting styles makes fascinating reading. She considers four different styles. These are:

1   warmth or nurturance
2   levels of expectation or maturity demands
3   the clarity and consistency of rules
4   the quality of communication between parents and child.

She blocked these into four parenting styles that she called:

1   The permissive style: this style is high in nurturance but low in maturity demands, control and communication.
2   The authoritarian style: this style is high in control and maturity demands, but low in nurturance and communication.
3   The authoritative style: this style is high in all four dimensions.
4   The neglecting or uninvolved type: this style is low in all four dimensions.

The permissive style

Children growing up with permissive parents tend to be lax in self-control. They do not readily take responsibility and as they are used to a great deal of freedom they can become aggressive when they have to obey someone else's rules. They tend to be immature because they have not been allocated tasks or been asked to conform to time limits. They find it hard to anticipate the outcomes of actions because this has not been required.

The authoritarian style

Families using an authoritarian style use high levels of control and maturity demands so the children must obey without demur and without conjuring up alternative ways of behaving. So problem solving and skills of independence are less likely to be developed. Low levels of warmth and responsiveness are also associated with children doing les well academically and socially. When children are held down in the home they may well react with impulsiveness/aggression once they taste freedom.

The authoritative style

The most positive style in terms of positive outcomes for all aspects of development e.g. relationships, emotional stability and intellectual development is the authoritative style. Children have higher self-esteem because they are listened to with respect and tasks are achievable with just the right amount of challenge. They are more independent but also more willing to be guided by parents. They are also more likely to show empathy to those less fortunate than themselves and their actions will be guided by moral reasoning.

The neglectful style

In this style the parents adopt a laissez-faire attitude and provide only basic requirements in contact and nurturance. As a result the children lack guidance and often make decisions about their education and welfare that bode ill for the future. They are more likely to experiment with drugs and feature more in the number of teenage pregnancies.

Bee (2004) makes an interesting comparison between toddlers and adolescents. She explains that two-year-olds and their parents survive the 'terrible twos' – a time when the toddlers are pushing for more independence while learning a bevy of new skills. In similar vein the adolescent is grappling with a new identity and may not have the skills to cope with the higher level of expectations that are part of the role. The drop in self-esteem at the start of adolescence is linked to this uncertainty. The two-year-old, kicking on the floor still uses mum or the parenting figure as a safe base and so do teenagers who use the family as a base from which to explore their world. Parents of both groups are striving for a balanced approach between giving too much freedom and being over restrictive. Bee also claims that in adolescence there is a reappearance of egocentricity. The teenager believes the world spins round him (as he did at age two), and there is also a feeling of invulnerability, which explains the teenagers' involvement in risky behaviour such as experimenting with drugs and having unprotected sex. But despite all this the bond remains to emerge more strongly as adolescence passes. One well-known phrase is apt: 'When I was fourteen I thought my father was really stupid – at eighteen I wondered how he had learned so much in such a short time!!'

Chapter 9

Programmes of activities

Touching and support

This is a difficult issue which needs to be discussed with school policy makers and certainly with parents. Children with dyspraxia have difficulty in feeling where their body parts are in space and so may not be able to respond to verbal instructions such as 'Lift your chin' or 'Hold your arms in to your sides'. And so teachers will gently adjust the position so that the child feels the correct alignment. This will probably have to happen on many occasions until the correct position is internalised. But with the current constraints on touching a child, how is this to be achieved? The answer may vary from region to region, but certainly it is critical that parents, head teachers and policy makers outside the school understand the nature of supporting the child, what it may involve and why it needs to be done. Perhaps if parents were allowed to see a demonstration of the kind of support that was envisaged, this would allay any fears. But with accusations of child abuse appearing more regularly, no teacher would want to be in a position where this could happen, so despite good relationships, it would be best to be clear about school policy and stay with it. In the past there was no problem with this kind of issue, but now, teachers and children need to be sure that all avenues of possible suspicion have been considered. The head teacher would need to be involved in any negotiation about support and probably written parental permission would need to be sought. Certainly those in authority need to be aware of the special issues which concern helping children with dyspraxia. It would be very sad if the no touching policy meant that help for the children was less effective than it could be.

Perceptual-motor programmes

The first thing to say is that many schools are convinced that their perceptual-motor programmes are helping children with dyspraxia. They speak of the children's increased confidence and competence in the hall and in tackling their daily routine. Of course it is not easy to prove that the programmes are the things that are causing the change. This could only be done if the children were in a laboratory with no extraneous influences to affect the test results. And as with any innovation, there have been some researchers who claim that such programmes are not working. Perhaps they have not been done regularly enough? Perhaps enough emphasis has not been put on the necessary standard and the activities have been rushed? Perhaps the children in some programmes were more severely disabled than in others? Perhaps too many children were taking part so that the teachers were not able to carry out the necessary observations? Perhaps the activities were not sufficiently linked to the specific difficulties the children displayed? Certainly more evaluative research needs to be done.

In the meanwhile, many teachers and parents claim that perceptual-motor programmes are the best things to offer as they can be done in school when the children are fresh; the children can be part of a group so they don't feel different in any way and the teachers who take the programmes are able to record careful observations of each child's progress. Certainly they will do no child any harm.

What should be included in a perceptual-motor programme?

Any of the activities which promote perceptual awareness and help develop the ability to move more effectively and efficiently can form part of a helpful programme. The activities should be chosen so that the children, with some effort and some practice, can be successful. A good standard of a simple movement pattern with understanding of *how* that standard was achieved is the main aim. It is important that the children recognise what they did, i.e. how their spontaneous and possibly inept efforts were altered to allow them to be successful. If this happens, there is more chance of the children being able to transfer or at least adapt these movements so that they are equally effective in different environments. A variety of activities help sustain interest and motivation and these can be chosen from:

- expressive movement activities, e.g dance and dance/drama;
- movements to promote kinaesthetic awareness, poise and balance;
- planning and organisational activities, e.g. problem solving challenges;
- ball skills.

Expressive movement activities

Lots of expressive movement gives a good start to the children with poor coordination, because in dance or drama types of activity, there is no need to control equipment as is the case with ball skills and there is no large apparatus to frighten nervous children as sometimes happens in gymnastic activities. The children have only to cope with their own bodies in space and some children find this quite enough.

This is a good medium for exploring rhythm which is very helpful in learning to remember movement patterns. Furthermore the freedom within expressive movement means that a rhythm can emerge as a dance or drama sequence is composed. No external rhythm dictates as happens when music or poetry acts as a stimulus – the intrinsic rhythm comes from the type of movement chosen and develops as children work together to compose a dance phrase. Most children enjoy composing a dance based on their own selection of action words, such as 'dashing together, swirling round, then gently sinking to the floor'. As the children show the qualities of the words through their expressive movement, an intrinsic rhythmic pattern emerges and with practice, they become able to say the action words as they dance.

Expressive movement can help the development of gross motor skills when sequences include the basic movement patterns. If they are given their expressive names, then as children experience the different qualities within the movements, their vocabulary develops too.

Example

Expressive movement patterns

Walking becomes creeping or sauntering or prowling or stalking, etc.

Running becomes dashing or darting or rushing or zipping.

Jumping becomes bounding or exploding or popping or leaping.

Gesturing becomes pointing or beckoning or turning or twisting or crumpling or stretching or sinking or growing, i.e. any action which happens on the spot.

Being still becomes freezing or holding or waiting or pausing.

If the teacher or the children themselves select one word from each type of action, they can be ordered into an expressive movement phrase. One example is shown in the box below.

Example

An expressive movement phrase

   Dash and freeze, crumple and pop pop pop!

Analysing the expressive content of that phrase shows that contrasts in speed and distance are built in and movements on the spot give the children time to 'get ready' for the next action phrase.

- Dash – moving quickly and lightly, skimming the floor for a short distance (to retain the quality of the action)
- Freeze – stopping suddenly with control, in a high position because of the next action
- Crumple – sinking slowly with either a rounded or jagged action. Gathering strength – on feet ready to
- Pop – exploding quickly, arms moving out from the centre of the body. Popping out to the original position ready to begin again. This might use three or four 'pops' depending on the available space.

The dance can be built into a duo with the children coming together and apart so that they develop an awareness of someone else's movement and adjust their timing and use of space to that. From duos, fours can come together to use the practised components and revamp their use of space and so compose a group dance, perhaps doing parts together or with some in sequence. Again awareness of other children, memorising the short dance and retaining the quality of the chosen movements provides an enjoyable challenge.

   The children should be encouraged to select actions which allow them to show contrasts for these blend easily and very satisfyingly into a rhythmical dance. Some other examples could be, 'swirl and hold, swirl and hold, creep away, creep away, pounce and freeze'.

   In this kind of phrase, words are repeated to give time for the intrinsic rhythm to be felt. If some children find swirling difficult, they can take quite a time on the 'hold' so that their balance is re-established ready for the next phrase.

To give the dancers more travelling space, the group can be subdivided and then the children who are watching try to guess the words the dancers are demonstrating, or some try to accompany the dance with percussion (not the music makers providing the stimulus for the dance because this would be another kind of experience where the rhythm was imposed). If this happens, then everyone is able to participate and learning words comes naturally alongside learning about the dance.

Dance drama

Once a bank of qualitative words are understood, acting out parts of stories can be fun, e.g. 'The giant stomped into the castle', or 'The tigers prowled through the long grass', for the younger ones, and 'The lightning flashed across the sky', or 'The smoke swirled from the bonfire', or 'The sea crashed onto the rocks', for the older group. The list is endless and after 'moving the words' the children should understand their meaning, where they might be applied and hopefully they will retain some to use in their storytelling or imaginative writing!

Activities for kinaesthetic/body awareness, poise and balance

It is vital that the children are constantly asked to feel a good sense of poise and extension as they move and when they are still, for this promotes body and spatial awareness. It also helps breathing which in turn helps movement to be controlled.

Begin and end each session by an activity which asks the children to think about the alignment of their body and where each part is in relation to the other parts.

Example

Stand well. Push the back of your head high. Think about your shoulders. Are they relaxed? Shrug your shoulders and let them go – and again. Swing your arms forward and back and hold your hands into your sides. Stretch up to the ceiling and out to the side – wide as you can – wiggle your fingers and bring them in to your sides again. Is everyone steady … and still … and standing well?

Sit down with your legs stretched out in front. Use your hands to help you balance. Can you sit tall? Are your shoulders level? Can you feel the back of your shoulders? Now spread your legs out wide and swoosh then together again – and again … who is still sitting tall? Look at your toes. Point them down to the floor and pull them back [the youngest ones love to say, 'Hello toes, goodbye toes' as they do this]. Now cross your legs over at your ankles. Make your toes point away and pull them back up. Change your legs over … Are you still sitting well?

Sideways rolling on mats is good for losing and regaining a sense of balance, but teachers should emphasise the long roll – 'Can you feel your toes as you roll? Push them out!' It is also important to let the children choose their own speed. Teachers should also check that the children are able to keep their arms into their sides so that elbows are not bumped.

This detail has been set out to show that the movement is basic but is to be done well with emphasis on the children knowing where their body parts are in relation to each other, where they are in space and how moving one part affects the others.

Activities to help planning/problem-solving activities

While all activities help 'doing' or the execution part of moving well, the other aspects, i.e. the organising and planning of movement, have also to be considered. To achieve this it is a good idea to think of the children building sequences of movement so that they get practice in remembering what comes next. In these activities, the main thrust is to have the children tell what they plan to do and how they are going to organise themselves or their equipment, e.g. 'I'll do this and then follow with that' kind of explanation or 'I'll put the bench near the box so that I can climb up …'. Teachers should encourage the children to do the movements well, but initially this would be less important than the implicit planning, resourcing and remembering the movements that they have chosen to do.

Have lots of estimating games, e.g. 'How many long steps will you need to place the ball in the box?' 'Which kind of ball will you choose if you are going to bounce a ball over the high skittle?' (Probably a foam one would not rise high enough, the children might not have the strength to put a basketball over, an airflow one would be difficult to control, so a volleyball might be the most successful.) The children can estimate and try!

Games can include 'space' words – 'Go *under* your partner's legs. Climb *through* the barrel, go *onto* the top of the box then jump down and come back to the start'.

Looking at Figure 9.1 a teacher needs to start with the aim – to get the beanbag or ball across the obstacle course and into the basket without losing it and without touching the obstacles on the way.

The teacher then asks 'How are you going to tackle this?'.

The child explains:

> I'll go *under* the rope,
> *through* the tunnels,
> *across* the boxes and put the beanbag,
> *up* and *into* the net.

Figure 9.1 Obstacle course

Adjustments can be made to add challenge for different ability levels:

- The obstacle course can be simplified or extra challenges can be added.
- Another child could guard the goal to add fun but make sure that the planning is thought through first.
- The child has to keep the ball moving as he goes (bouncing the ball or dribbling a football or rolling the ball round the body).
- Other children are the obstacles – perhaps sitting using their legs as scissors so that the child had to judge when to get through the barricade.

NB Even when the teacher would seem to do all the planning, e.g 'move along the bench on your back head first', there is still a lot of 'child thinking' involved in getting the movement done.

More favourite games and activities to help fine motor skills

1 Simon says 'Do this', 'Do that'

This helps copying, listening skills and body awareness. Teachers need to be sympathetic with the speed of the instructions – perhaps giving a warning 'mmmmm' before 'do that' so that the dyspraxic children have extra time to prepare.

2 Any poems or songs which have actions, e.g 'Incy wincy spider', 'Heads, shoulders, knees and toes', or 'In a cottage in a wood'

These games can be enjoyed by the older children if they are in a mixed age group and they feel they are showing or helping the younger ones. They are very good for finger dexterity and fitting the speed of the actions to the speed of the song.

3 Pass the parcel games

These help laterality, i.e. an awareness of 'passing to the side' and fine motor skills when the parcel has to be unwrapped. The children can sit and push the parcel round with their feet as one progression. This is difficult but fun for a brief spell.

4 Playing the piano or keyboard

This is very good for coordination and finger strengthening and dexterity.

5 'Angels in the snow'

Children lie flat on floor on their backs:

(a) Sweep arms and legs wide, then together – at the same time.
(b) Sweep one arm and leg on the same side, then the opposite side, wide and together.
(c) Have children lying on their backs in a circle, fingertips touching to make an angel design. Other children, not those with dyspraxia, can run over the outstretched legs. With agile children the angels can be moving their limbs but ensure that they can follow a steady rhythm.

This is a very good way of helping children feel where the backs of all their body parts are. Old clothes help!

6 Guess the number of sweets or cubes in a jar

Unscrew the lid, tip them out and fill the jar again – minus one sweet for the guesser!

Holding the jar with one hand and unscrewing the lid is very difficult. At first the children will clamp the jar into their bodies for extra support but with practice should be able to hold it on the table to unscrew the lid.

7 Wind a lace round a bobbin

This is very difficult – a real test of fine motor skill. All sorts of threading activities can act as precursors of this one!

8 Touching, feeling

In twos children have to name parts that are being touched. The challenge is when they have to close their eyes so that feeling rather than seeing becomes the important sense.

9 Guess the letter or number

In twos, one child draws letters or figures on a partner's back. The partner has to guess what they are.

This can be made into a game where half the class sit in a circle with their eyes closed. The other half creep in unseen and draw their own initial on the backs. The sitting child has to guess who it is.

10 All sorts of copying activities helping awareness of others, and spatial patterning

Sit facing child with two hands raised in front of each person. Draw a circle with one hand keeping the other one still. Draw a circle with the other hand. Try both hands. Progression: draw a figure of 8.

Copying is very helpful for both spatial awareness and tracking skills. Note the children's ability to track the demonstrated pattern. Gently hold their heads still if there is a lot of head turning. This encourages side vision and strengthens the muscles controlling the eyes. Try when sitting then standing.

Copying circular patterns

11 Drawing names in the air – with one hand then the other

For fun, hip mobility and control, the children can lie on their backs and draw their names with their toes!

12 Hoops

Lifting hoops over heads and climbing through – pass hoop to partner who puts feet in first then lifts it overhead – reverse.

Build speed up into a smooth circling action.

13 Skipping rope

In twos, turning a large rope. Children with difficulties to be on one end only. Other children try to run through.

Activities to help ball skills

The main ball skills are:

- rolling
- retrieving
- throwing
- catching
- aiming.

Activities to help ball skills

1 Rolling and retrieving

Tunnels – in twos facing one another. Sitting legs outstretched and apart. Roll the ball into the gap made by the other person's legs. Then twos join up to form a circle in the same sitting position. The child with the ball chooses where to roll it and the receiver rolls the ball on into the next tunnel.

This activity helps directionality, it's fun and the speed can be varied. The good thing is that no time is lost chasing the ball to bring it back. It is firmly trapped in the different tunnels! Watch out for children having difficulty in releasing the ball and if this happens substitute a larger ball.

Rolling a ball ahead and retrieving it before it reaches a line on the floor. This involves the child running round and fielding the ball in a 'basket'.

Roll the ball against an upturned bench and retrieve it on the rebound. The actions must be quicker this time or at least they must be adjusted to suit the strength of the roll.

2 Throwing and catching

3 Throw and catch sympathetically with a partner

Aim for ten throws without dropping the ball. Although this sounds easy, children with poor three dimensional vision will turn away rather than catch. Use a foam ball and judge how much space should be between the children. Progress to throwing 'out to the side' or lower or higher so that the throwing child must plan and the receiving child must anticipate and adjust.

Use a variety of balls as skill improves. Foam balls travel more slowly and are easily retrieved, but they don't have much 'go'. Volleyballs are best because they are the 'real thing' but are light enough not to hurt.

4 In threes, 'Donkey in the middle'

Change donkey frequently and limit the area where each can go.

5 Fivers

In threes, pass from the middle to the side and back to the middle. The middle person, O, has the ball. He throws to X who throws it back. O then turns to face X1, throws the ball, receives it back and then turns to face X again. The throw is repeated to X who catches it and the two change places. This is the first sequence of five throws. X in the centre is now facing X1 and the five throws continue with the children changing places until the original positions are regained. The trio sit down to show they have completed the game. Once the routine is established the game can be a competition to see which group of three children finishes first. Having the threes lined across the hall means that all groups have the same distance to throw! This game may need to be built up slowly. It is a very good one for helping planning, for back in the classroom the children can draw out the path of the ball, numbering each throw.

6 Throwing the ball against a wall

Lots of throwing the ball against a wall and catching the rebound gives practice in judging speed, distance and direction.

7 Aiming

'Skittle alley' – rolling the ball to knock down skittles helps aiming. Some children can bowl the ball, others can be in charge of replacing the skittles, others can keep the score. This can be called ten pin bowling if 'alleys' are constructed. Skittles can be made with plastic bottles half-filled with sand. Younger children can make lighter skittles which will topple more easily.

'Aiming high' – wicker waste paper baskets tied to wallbars are marvellous for learning to aim into a basket. If these are not available, sometimes netball stands can be lowered. The action involves an overhand push and so it is important to establish the correct stance, i.e. having the opposing foot forward. Judging speed, distance and direction are all important.

Including different age groups

Most activities can suit any age group if simple alterations are made, e.g. a five-year-old could use a beanbag for throwing and catching but an eleven-year-old would probably want to work with a ball. There are many sorts of balls, from foam ones which are light and don't travel too fast but don't bounce either to hedgehog balls which are hard but help children to grip. Volleyballs are much better than the heavier basketballs as they don't hurt if catches are missed and faces get bumped. So lots of variety in the apparatus gives different levels of challenge to the same task.

Similarly, difficulties can be added by changing the environment – perhaps adding more apparatus, more things to remember or perhaps having distracting movements or noises! If children have to walk along a pathway, difficulty is increased if the pathway is curved or angled or if obstacles are placed in the way so that they have to 'step over' or 'go round'. These require the children to adjust their pattern and balance demands are increased – the child will have to balance on one foot if 'stepping over' is part of the task and this can be challenging if the child tries to 'keep tall' as the adjustment is made.

Differences in speed add challenge, e.g. 'Can you throw the ball against the wall and catch it cleanly five times before I say stop?', and this can be made really tricky if someone else counts out the 1, 2, 3, 4, 5 rhythm. To experience this, ask someone to clap a regular beat and then skip down the room to it. The person clapping mustn't look and follow *your* rhythm – you must follow theirs! Other challenges can be made by altering the steepness of an inclined bench or asking children to carry out movement patterns together, e.g. 'Watch your partner as you walk along the benches and keep level'.

A final point is to remind teachers that the point of this programme is to help the children cope. Teachers are not to expect high level skill performance. A small number of basic exercises carefully chosen to help each child's profile of needs, done well and practised regularly, will suffice. Although the activities may not seem very challenging, they will stretch children with difficulties, i.e. those who can find it difficult to do things rhythmically and/or in sequence, so that an effective and efficient pattern without extraneous movements results. They have been chosen to improve the children's basic movement patterns which will hopefully give them confidence and competence throughout their day. It is a very good plan for teachers to try the movements themselves first to feel the demands made by an activity when it is done well. Good luck!

And so there are many fun ways to help children with dyspraxia. Building activities so that the balance, rhythm, timing and directionality demands gradually increase will help the children's self-awareness to develop and enable them to become more confident and competent children across the curriculum and in all the other coping skills they require at home. With a positive mentor, with practice and determination these children will soon, or perhaps a little later, be able to say, 'Look at me, I can do it too!'

A movement observation record

Child's name ....

Age .... years .... months .... Sex   Male □   Female □

This checklist is for one child who is causing you concern. Please record the child's usual level of competence rather than focusing on one unusual occurrence. If, however, the child's movement is erratic, making a general picture difficult or less than useful, please say that this is the case.

Before looking more specifically at motor development, please say whether you would consider that this was the child's only area of difficulty or whether there are other problems too.

Please tick if appropriate and add any other area of concern.

Does the child have:	Yes	No
(a) poor sight?	□	□
(b) low hearing?	□	□
(c) a physical disability?	□	□
(d) difficulty in understanding instructions?	□	□
(e) speech difficulties?	□	□
(f) body-build problems:	□	□
(i) very overweight?	□	□
(ii) fragile?	□	□
(iii) little strength?	□	□

And is the child:	Yes	No
(g) very tense and unsure?	□	□
(h) aggressive?	□	□
(i) lethargic – hard to interest?	□	□
(j) lacking persistence?	□	□
(k) seeking attention all the time?	□	□

Any other difficulty? Please note below.

The checklist now asks you to tick one box for each competence then give a mark out of 10 for 'general coping ability' in that field. The boxes are 'yes, can do it'; 'some difficulty', meaning that the child needs real effort to cope; 'severe difficulty', meaning that the child does not cope and 'regression' which means that the child's performance is getting worse.

NB: This is a movement observation record to help teachers compile Assessment Profiles for school use or for gaining access to specialist help. It is not a test to determine dyspraxia.

Gross motor skills

Can the child:	Yes can do it	Some difficulty	Severe difficulty	Regression	Please give details
(a) stand still, balanced and in control?					
(b) sit still retaining poise?					
(c) walk smoothly and with good poise?					
(d turn corners efficiently?					
(e) walk on tip-toe with control (count of 6)?					
(f) jump (two feet off floor)?					
(g) kick a stationary ball?					
(h) catch a large soft ball when thrown sympathetically?					
(i) roll sideways and recover to stand with agood sense of timing and balance?					
(j) crawl?					

Give a mark out of 10 for coordination in gross motor skills.

Fine motor skills

Can the child:	Yes can do it	Some difficulty	Severe difficulty	Regression	Please give details
(a) use a pencil/paint brush with control?					
(b) pick up and replace objects efficiently?					
(c) use two hands together to thread beads, build Lego or do jigsaws?					
(d) draw a person with some detail of parts?					
(e) dress in the correct order?					

Give a mark out of 10 for dexterity in fine motor skills. ☐

Intellectual skills

Can the child:	Yes can do it	Some difficulty	Severe difficulty	Regression	Please give details
(a) talk readily to adults?					
(b) talk readily to children?					
(c) articulate clearly?					
(d) use a wide vocabulary?					
(e) listen attentively?					
(f) respond appropriately?					

(f) follow a sequence of instructions?					
(g) understand: i) spatial concepts – over, under, through? ii) simple mathematical concepts – bigger, smaller?					

Give the child a mark out of 10 for intellectual skills. ☐

Social skills

Does the child:	Usually	Sometimes	Rarely	Regression	Please give details
(a) take turns with no fuss?					
(b) interact easily with other children?					
(c) take the lead in activities?					
(d) participate in someone else's game?					

Give the child a mark out of 10 for social skills. ☐

Emotional skills

Does the child:	Usually	Sometimes	Rarely	Regression	Please give details
(a) appear confident in following the daily routine?					
(b) constantly seek attention?					
(c) disturb other children?					
(d sustain eye contact?					
(e) cope in new situations?					
(f) appear aggressive or defiant?					
(g) withdraw easily?					
(h) show impulsive behaviour?					

Give the child a mark out of 10 for emotional skills.   ☐

This record could usefully be shared with other teachers, with physiotherapists, occupational therapists or psychologists, i.e. with anyone who has resources to help the child.

Activities to help ball skills

The main ball skills are:

Rolling and retrieving, throwing and catching, aiming and kicking.

There are many kinds of balls to try. Foam ones don't hurt. Volleyballs are great because they are the 'real thing' but are light enough not to hurt.

1   Tunnels:
    In twos facing one another. Sitting legs ball is outstretched and apart. Roll the ball into the gap made by the other person's legs.

    Then twos join up into sixes or eights.

Try lots of rolling so that tracking the practised, e.g. rolling a tennis ball into an upturned bucket. This helps aiming skills.

    In groups, sit in a circle in the same position. The child with the ball chooses where to roll it and the receiver rolls the ball on into the next tunnel.

This helps directionality, it's fun and the speed can be varied. The good thing is that no time is lost chasing the ball to bring it back. It is firmly held in the tunnel.

2   Rolling a ball ahead and retrieving it before it reaches a line on the floor.

This helps judging speed, i.e. estimating the pace in line with the ability to catch up.

    Roll the ball against an upturned bench and retrieve it on the rebound.

Again judging the speed is important. Good for varying pace.

3   Throw underarm sympathetically to partner. Aim for 10 throws without dropping the ball.

Although this sounds easy, children with poor three dimensional vision will turn away rather than catch. Use a foam ball. Work on the throwing arm having a smooth sweep. Say 'throw' at the moment of release if this is difficult.

4   Catching – as above but emphasise watching the ball and having a basket ready to catch.

The alternate foot to the throwing arm should be forward to let the arm move easily. Aim for accuracy, not distance.

5   In threes, 'Donkey in the middle'. Change 'donkey' frequently.

6 'Skittle alley' (rolling and aiming):
Rolling the ball to knock down skittles helps aiming – can be related to ten pin bowling if 'alleys' are constructed.

Use a variety of balls as skill improves. Foam balls travel more slowly and are easily retrieved, but they don't have much 'go'.

This activity helps timing of releasing the ball. It gives lots of satisfaction when the skittles fall. Younger children can make skittles from plastic bottles, half-filled with dry sand and these will topple more easily than the gym ones which are hard to knock over.

7 Throwing and aiming:
Begin with a large target so that the child concentrates on the throwing action and keep the distance short to begin with. Once this is established use waste paper baskets for targets and gradually raise the height. This links with basketball and netball.

This probably needs an overarm throw if the basket is even at waist height. It is important to take this slowly. Hold the ball at shoulder level in the preferred hand. Support it with the other hand.

8 Kicking:
1 Sit on a chair. Have the ball ahead of the kicking foot. Push the ball into a wide goal.

Aim for control of the body as a kicking action can throw the body offbalance if it is too fierce. Use the word 'push' rather than 'kick'. The children have to control the direction of the ball so goal posts make the activity real and great fun.

2 Stand with support, e.g. between two chairs. Push ball into goal. Gradually remove support and reduce size of goal.

3 Take two steps, begin RF (if preferred foot) LF and kick with RF.

Have the alternate foot forward, the body twisting to the ball side. Encourage 'pushing' the ball till the action is steady.

4 Gradually use more walking steps then increase speed. Keep ball stationary. Gradually have ball moving so that the child has to judge the timing and the speed of the ball in relation to the action of the foot.

5 In twos kicking the ball to each other sympathetically. Use the inside of the foot to control the ball and push it to make the pass accurate.

6 Have a donkey in the middle game as for throwing. Build up to a two against two game.

Appendix 3

Games and activities to help fine motor skills

1	Simon says 'Do this', 'Do that'.	Teacher as Simon makes different body shapes. Children copy when 'Simon says do this' but hold still on 'do that'.
2	Any poems or songs which have actions, e.g. 'Incy wincy spider', In a cottage in a wood'.	Helps finger dexterity. Remember to give support if children are sitting on the floor.
3	Pass the parcel games.	Helps laterality – awareness of children to the side helped by passing action. Finger dexterity helped by receiving and letting the parcel go – and by pulling off the paper if this is part of the game.
4	Playing the piano or keyboard.	Marvellous for finger dexterity and control.
5	'Angels in the snow': Children lie flat on floor. Sweep arms and legs wide, then together. Have children lying in a circle to make a star design. Older children, not those with dyspraxia, can run over the outstretched legs. With agile children the angels can be moving their limbs but ensure that they can follow a steady rhythm.	Helps body awareness of the back of the body, back of arms and legs. Helps rhythm and needs concentration.
6	Guess the number of sweets or cubes in a jar. Unscrew the lid, tip them out and fill the jar again – minus one sweet for the winner!	Helps finger strength and two-handed coordination. Helps crossing the midline. A good activity for helping everyday coping skills at home.
7	Wind a lace round a bobbin.	This is difficult as one hand has to be still while the other is moving.
8	In twos, children have to name parts that are being touched.	This helps body awareness and assessment of sensitivity to touch.

From Christine Macintyre (2009), *Dyspraxia 5–14*. London: Routledge. © 2009 Christine Macintyre.

9 In twos, one child draws letters or figures on the other's back. The other has to guess what they are.

This can be made into a game where half the class sit in a circle with their eyes closed. The other half creep in unseen and draw their own initial on the backs. The sitting child has to guess who it is. Try sitting then standing.

10 All sorts of copying activities help awareness of others, and spatial patterning.

Note the children's ability to track the pattern. Gently hold their heads still if there is a lot of head turning. This encourages side vision.

Sit facing child with two hands raised in front of each person. Draw a circle with one hand keeping the other one still. Draw a circle with the other hand. Try both hands.

Progression: draw a figure of 8.

Vary the size of the figure 8.

11 Drawing names in the air – with one hand then the other. For fun and mobility lie on back and draw names with toes!

Helps mobility – not suitable for children with poor muscle tone in the shoulder girdle.

12 Lifting hoops over heads and climbing through – pass hoop to partner who puts feet in first then lifts it over head – reverse.

Good for planning timing of actions. Do it slowly first to feel the rhythm. Watch for any unnecessary hand flapping as the child waits to receive the hoop.

Build speed up into a smooth circling action.

13 In twos, turning a large rope. Children with difficulties to be on one end only. Other children try to run through.

Activities to help gross motor skills

WALKING

Rope or coloured tape on the floor. If there is extra hand fluttering, a beanbag in each hand can help the children feel the position of their hands.

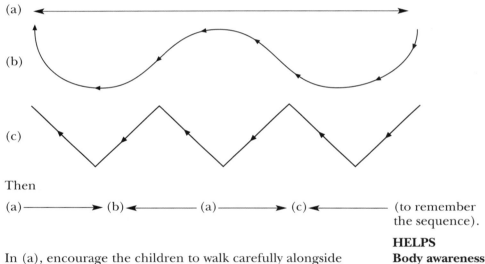

Then

(a) ——————→ (b) ◄———— (a) ——————→ (c) ◄———— (to remember the sequence).

HELPS

In (a), encourage the children to walk carefully alongside the line, not necessarily on it, with a heel–toe action.

Body awareness

(b) and (c) are more challenging due to the gentle then acute changes of direction.

Propulsion

Encourage the children to move carefully and slowly, emphasising walking tall.

Good posture

Progression 1: two children begin at different places and watch each other, aiming to finish at the same time.

Timing

Progression 2: substitute crawling in (a). This is very important for coordination and vital if there is no climbing equipment.

CRAWLING

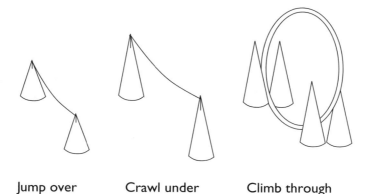

Jump over   Crawl under   Climb through

Add several hoops to crawl through.

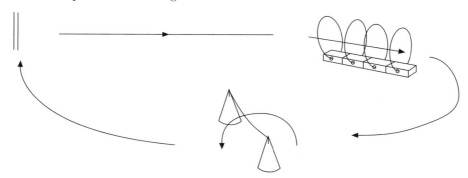

Children try not to touch the hoops.
Emphasise 'through', 'under' and then 'over'.

Encourage children to call out directions as they move.

Progression: children rearrange apparatus and remember
spatial concepts. Older children can crawl along a box
top – two sections only – remember they have to 'crawl
down' back to the floor.

HELPS
Coordination
Directionality

Conceptual
understanding of
spatial terms

Development of
ordering

CRAWLING AND CLIMBING

Crawl over a soft rolled up mat (carpet).
Crawl/climb up steps or plank (no hands as progression).
Jump down into a good space and run round to begin again.

HELPS

Sequencing

Climbing actions using the recovery to aid the preparation of the next action

Progression: bunny jump over rolled carpet.

Strengthening wrists (weight bearing)

This is a good visual sequence of activities.

Emphasise standing well (pushing the back of the head up) to begin and finish.

MARCHING AND WAITING

It is important that the following activities are done calmly and carefully with no rush! Standing tall gives an important sense of poise and body awareness.

Rhythmical awareness

March forward smartly for four steps and 'wait, wait, wait'.

Control

March backwards for four steps and 'wait, wait, wait'.

Listening skills

Repeat adding a clap on the wait.

Body awareness (marching tall, heads high)

Teacher counts out rhythmically:

1 2 3 4 and wait, wait, wait
Back 2 3 4 and wait, wait, wait
Forward 2 3 4 and clap, clap, clap
Back 2 3 4 and clap, clap, clap.

Rhythm through counting to 4

Awareness of other children as they keep in line

Progression:
(a)

Laterality (awareness of sidedness)

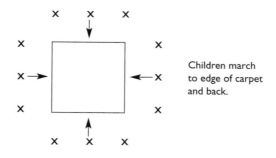

Children march to edge of carpet and back.

All children repeat the pattern they have already learned at the same time, perhaps substituting waving for clapping for the younger ones. Older children could clap hands with the children opposite. This would be rhythmically challenging.

HELPS

(b) Children on opposite sides go in and out at different times.

Judging size of step

Allow children to march heavily if this helps some get good feedback.

JUMPING

Feet together.

Free jumping, feet together to build consecutive actions:

Jump and jump and wait, jump and jump and wait.
use arm swing to help propulsion forward.

Progression:

Coordination

Strong leg action

Continuous movement

3 coloured hoops

Jump into hoops – 'jump and jump and jump and out'; varying distance. Work for control and rhythm.

Planning and sequencing

(Some children will need to 'shuffle' to regain a good preparatory position for the next jump, while others will 'jack-in-the-box'.)

One child per large hoop.

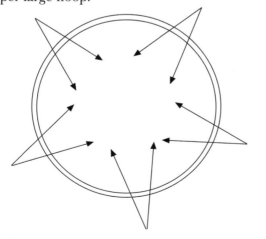

Leg strength

Control

Coordination

Rhythmic development

From Christine Macintyre (2009), *Dyspraxia 5–14*. London: Routledge. © 2009 Christine Macintyre.

Jumping in and out in all directions.

HELPS

Teacher can accompany with tambourine. 1 and 2 and 3 and 4 (jumps).

Rest, get ready – now you're off. 1 and 2 and 3 and 4 and stand quite still and tall.

NEGOTIATING

Arrange bricks into paths.

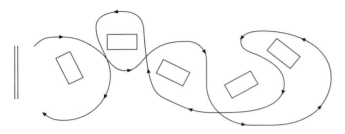

Children have to stay just a whisper away but not touching, then run back. Children choose running, skipping, hopping, moving backwards.

Spatial awareness

Body boundary

Progression:
Bowl hoop or dribble football.
Replace bricks with chairs.
Rearrange pathway.

Control and manipulation skills

HOPPING

Hopping over line (say six hops), RF (or preferred foot).

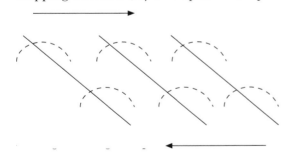

Balance

Coordination

Body awareness

Partner awareness

Progression:

Two children approach at the same time, hopping four or six times.
Bend down to touch other child's foot (hands on floor).

Regain standing.
Change foot to hop back.

HELPS

BALANCING

Walking along broad side of bench – head high, looking forward.

Progression 1:

Hold hoop above head as you walk. Keep hoop steady!

Progression 2:

Walking along narrow ledge of bench, with light handhold
where necessary. Then alone – trying to feel for position
of next step rather than looking down.

Progression 3:

See-saw – two benches sit astride as see-saw.
Teacher supervision required.

Progression 4:

Single bench broad side up.
One foot flat on broad side of bench. Push head high,
come down to floor, push high, repeat.
Keep the same foot on the bench till the end.
Repeat using other foot on bench.

Progression 5:

Use the same activity but the narrow side of the bench.
Offer some light support so that the child feels the extension.
Emphasise strong straight back and legs.

Balance

Coordination

Timing

Partner cooperation

Good poise

Body awareness

Leg strengthening

Balance

Segmented movement

Body awareness

Coordination

Progression 6:   **HELPS**

Using either the broad or narrow side of the bench as
appropriate – stand well, balance on one foot, arms outstretched.

Draw as large a circle as possible with the other foot (allow time
between turns to correct any overbalancing).
Change over so that circling foot becomes balancing foot.

Bunny jumps:

1   Freely on floor, emphasising weight evenly balanced on   **Transfer of
    two hands looking forward and up.   weight from feet
                                                                     on to strong
2   Over tape/rope or through hoop (trying not to touch hoop).   arms**

Progression for most agile children: **Weight-bearing
                                                                    strengthening
Child A holds hoop just above floor level.   for arms/hands**
Child B bunny jumps through, Child A moving hoop to clear
feet.

From Christine Macintyre (2009), *Dyspraxia 5–14*. London: Routledge. © 2009 Christine Macintyre.

Useful addresses

AFASIC (Association for all Speech Impaired
   Children)
347 Central Markets
Smithfield
London
EC1A 9NH
Tel No 020 7236 3632

British Dyslexia Foundation
98 London Road
Reading
Berkshire
Tel No 01189 662677

Dyspraxia Foundation
8 West Alley
Hitchin
Hertfordshire
SG5 lEG
Tel No 01462 455016
Helpline 01462 454986

Healthcall Discovery Centre
12 Cathedral Road
Cardiff
CF9 1LJ
Tel No 02920 222011
Fax No 02920 666850

I–Can
4 Dyer's Building
Holborn
London
EC1N 2QP
Tel No 0870 010 4066

National Autistic Society
393 City Road
Stratford
London
EC1V 1NG
Tel No 020 7833 2299
Helpline 0870 600 8585

The Nuffield Centre Dyspraxia Programme
Nuffield Hearing & Speech Centre
RNTNE Division of Royal Free
Hamsptead NHS Trust
Grays Inn Road
London
WCIX 8DA
Tel No 020 7915 1535

Parents for Inclusion
Unit 20
70 South Lambeth Road
London
SW8 1RL
Tel No 020 7735 7735
Helpline 020 7582 5008

Scottish Dyslexia Association
Unit 3
Stirling Business Centre
Wellgreen
Stirling
FK8 2DZ
Tel No 01786 446650

Bibliography

Aboud, F.E. and Doyle, A.B. (2005) 'The development of in group pride in black Canadians', *Journal of Cross Cultural Psychology*, **26**.

Ainsworth, M.D.S. (1972) 'Attachment and dependency: A comparison', in J.L. Gewirtz (ed.) *Attachment and Dependency*. Washington DC: V.H. Winston.

American Psychiatric Association (1994) *Developmental Coordination Disorder Diagnostic and Statistical Manual*. Washington DC: APA.

Ayres, J.A. (1972) *Sensory Integration and Learning Disorders*. Los Angeles: Western Psychological Services.

Baumrind, D. (1972) 'Socialisation and instrumental competence in young children', in *The Young Child: Reviews of research*, Vol. 2, 202–224. Washington DC: National Association for the Education of Young Children.

Bee, H. (1999) *Lifespan Development*. New York: HarperCollins College Publishers.

Bee, H. (2007) *The Developing Child*. New York: HarperCollins College Publishers.

Bee, H. (2004) *The Growing Child*, 2nd edn. London: Longman Publishers.

Blythe, P. (1992) 'A physical approach to resolving learning difficulties'. Paper presented at the 4th European Conference of Neuro-developmental Delay in Children: Chester.

Bruner, J. (1966) *The Process of Education*. Cambridge, MA: Harvard University Press.

Byrne, B. (2003) 'Countering bullying behaviour: A proactive approach'. Paper presented at Galway Education Centre, March 2003.

Carter, R. (2000) *Mapping the Mind*. London: Phoenix Publications.

Chesson R. *et al* (1990) *The Child with Motor/Learning Difficulties*. Aberdeen: Royal Aberdeen Children's Hospital.

Child, D. (1986) *Psychology and the Teacher*. 4th edn. London: Holt Reinhart & Winston.

Cole, D.A. (1991) 'Change in self-perceived competence as a function of peer and teacher evaluation', *Developmental Psychology*, **27**, 682–88.

Cooley, C. (1962) *Human Nature and the Social Order*. New York: Charles Scribner.

Cotrell, S. (1992) *The Effects of Obstetric Problems on Neuro-developmental Delay*. 4th European Conference on Developmental Delay, March 1992.

Cowden, J.E. and Eason, B.L. (1991) 'Pediatric adapted physical education', *Adapted Physical Activity Quarterly*, **8**, 263–79.

Dyspraxia Foundation (1998) *Praxis Makes Perfect II*. Hitchin: Dyspraxia Foundation.

Eisenberg, N. (1992) *The Caring Child*. Cambridge, MA: Harvard University Press.

Fagot, B.I. and Pears, K.C. (1996) 'Changes in attachment during the third year: Consequences and predictions', *Development and Psychopathology*, **8**.

Farnham-Diggory S. (1992) *The Learning Disabled Child*. Cambridge, MA: Harvard University Press.

French, J. and Lee, M. (1996) Cited in G. Reid (ed.) 'Developmental dyspraxia: An overview', in *Dimensions of Dyslexia*, Vol. 2. Edinburgh: Moray House Institute.

Garmezy, N. (1993) 'Vulnerability and resilience', in D.C. Funder, R.D. Parke, C. Tomlinson-Keasey and K. Wideman (eds) *Studying Lives through Time: Personality and Development*. Washington DC: American Psychological Association, 377–98.

Gecas, V. and Seff , M.A. (1990) 'The family and adolescents'. *Journal of Marriage and the family*, 52, 941–958.

Gessell, A. (1925) *The Mental Growth of the Preschool Child*. New York: Macmillan.

Goddard Blythe, S. (2005) *The Well Balanced Child*. Stroud: Hawthorn Press.

Goddard Blythe, S. (2008) *What Babies and Children Really Need*. Stroud: Hawthorn Press.

Gurney, P. (1987) 'Self-esteem enhancement in children: A review of research findings', *Educational Research*, **29**(2).

Harris, P. (1992) *Children and Emotion: The Development of Psychological Understanding*. Oxford: Blackwell.

Harter, S. (1990) 'Processes underlying adolescent self-concept formation', in R. Montemayor, G.R. Adams and T.P. Gulotta (eds) *From Childhood to Adolescence: A Transitional Period?* Newbury Park, CA: Sage.

Kirby, A. (1999a) 'What should we call children's coordination problems? Developmental Coordination Disorder or Dyspraxia?' *Dyspraxia Review*.

Kirby, A. (1999b) *Dyspraxia: The Hidden Handicap*. London: Souvenir Press.

Lerner, R.M. (2005) 'Adolescent maturational changes and psychosocial development: A dynamic interactional perspective', *Journal of Youth and Adolescence*, **14**, 355–72.

Levitt, M., Weber, R.A. and Guacci, J.L. (1993) 'Convoys of social support in childhood and early adolescence'. *Developmental Psychology*, **29**.

Lewis, N. (2005) 'Social knowledge and social development', *Merrill-Palmer Quarterly*, **36**, 93–116.

Lucas, A. *et al.* (1992) 'Breast milk and subsequent intelligence quotient in children born prematurely', *Lancet*, **339**, 261–64.

Maccoby, E.E. (1990) *Social Development, Psychological Growth and the Parents–Child Relationship*. New York: Harcourt Brace Janovich.

Macintyre, C. and Arrowsmith, J. (1988) *The Assessment of Motor Patterns*. Edinburgh: Dunfermline College of Physical Education.

Macintyre, C, (2000a) *Dyspraxia in the Early Years*. London: David Fulton Publishers.

Macintyre, C. (2000b) *The Art of Action Research in the Classroom*. London: David Fulton Publishers.

McClelland, D. and Kinsey, S. (1996) 'Mixed age grouping helps children develop social skills and a sense of belonging', *The Magnet Newsletter* **5**(1).

Murray, M. and Keene, C. (1998) *The ABC of Bullying*. Dublin: Mercier Press.

Pettit, G.S. *et al.* (1996) 'Stability and change in peer-rejected status: The role of child behaviour, parenting and family ecology', *Merrill-Palmer Quarterly* **42**, 295–318.

Pope, M. (1988) 'Dyspraxia: A head teacher's perspective', in *Praxis Makes Perfect*. Hitchin: The Dyspraxia Trust.

Portwood, M. (1998) *Developmental Dyspraxia, Identification and Intervention: A Manual for Parents and Professionals*. London: David Fulton Publishers.

Portwood, M. (2004) 'Dyspraxia', in A. Lewis and B. Norwich (eds) *Special Teaching for Special Children: Pedagogies for Inclusion*. Oxford: Oxford University Press.

Reid, G (2005) 'Specific learning difficulties: The spectrum'. In Nichola Jones (ed.) *Developing School Provision for Children with Dyspraxia*. Edinburgh: Paul Chapman.

Rush, P. (1997) *Managing the Dyspraxic Child Through Sensory Integration Therapy*. Conference presentation: Appleford School, Shrewton.

Schaffer, E.J. (1989) 'Dimensions of mother–infant interaction: measurement stability and predictive validity', *Infant Behaviour and Development* **12**.

Scottish Consultative Council on the Curriculum (1999) *Promoting Learning: Assessing Children's Progress*, 3–5.

Smoll, F.L. and Schultz, R.W. (2006) 'Quantifying gender differences in physical performance: A developmental perspective'. *Developmental Psychology* 26, 360–69.

Sugden, D.A. and Henderson, S.E. (1994) 'Help with movement', *Special Children* **75**: *Back to Basics*, 13.

Sweeney, C. (2007) *Good Inclusive Practice for Children with Dyspraxia in Irish Primary Schools*. Dublin: Ell Publishing.

Steinberg, L. (1988) *You and Your Adolescent: A Parents' Guide for Ages 10–20*. New York: Harper and Row.

Taylor, A. (2007) *Preparing for Adolescence*. Dyspraxia Foundation: Nottingham.

Vygotsky, L.S. (1978) *Mind and Society*. Cambridge, MA: Harvard University Press.

Winston, R. (2004) *The Human Mind*. London: Bantam Books.

Wood, D. (1998) *How Children Think and Learn*. Buckingham: Open University Press.

Index